The Rowboat Revisited

Sailing Through Life In A Rowboat - II

Connie L. Hawkins

The Rowboat Revisited

ISBN: 978-0-9787472-2-0
Printed in the United States of America
©2008 by Connie L. Hawkins

Cover and interior design by Isaac Publishing, Inc.

*The quotes used in this book are taken from the
Book of Unusual Quotations
Selected and edited by Rudolf Flesch
Published by Harper & Row – New York, Evanston and London
Copyright 1957*

Accent Publications
An imprint of Isaac Publishing, Inc.
P.O. 342
Three Rivers, MI 49093
www.isaacpublishing.com

No part of this book may be reproduced or transmitted in any form or by any means, electronic or mechanical—including photocopying, recording, or by any information storage and retrieval system—without permission in writing from the publisher, except as provided by United States of America copyright law.

Please direct your inquiries to admin@isaacpublishing.com

This book is dedicated to Marilyn, Lisa and Julie – all a great encouragement to me both in my personal life and in my writing. Throughout the years, even when I have messed up, they have never let me down and still continue to love me – just like God loves me and for that I am most thankful.

And to my mother who taught me what I needed to know in order to survive life; may she rest in peace. To my father for his support of my various writing projects over the years. And to Mary Tweksbury for her help in editing and promoting this book!

The Rowboat Revisited

Sailing through Life in a Rowboat –Again!

Sailing to me is to begin a journey by water, usually in a sailing vessel of some sort, in my case, a rowboat. Those skilled at the art of sailing might say, to navigate the high seas is to float along in an effortless way. This is not so in my situation. Everything I do in life seems to require a great deal of effort.

To realize that a sail is a mere piece of cloth makes the idea of sailing a bit unnerving unless you have an excellent ship mate at the helm.

Sailing through life in a rowboat is no easy task; at least it hasn't been for me. If I didn't have Christ at the controls I'm sure the boat would have sunk years ago.

What I've learned about sailing through life:

Sailing is a lot more fun when you have someone in the boat with you.

It helps a great deal if you're both rowing in the same direction!

Sailing demands physical and emotional strength.

Sailing takes wit, know how and fortitude.

Sailing for me, any way, requires a lot of fortitude and a bucket (I'll explain that part of the story later).

To sail through life in a rowboat takes courage.

"We do all stand in the front ranks of battle every moment of our lives; where there is a brave man (or woman) there is the thickest of the fight, there the post of honor."   *—Henry David Thoreau*

And so in that post of honor I sail again through life in a rowboat, hoping as I sail to entertain you with stories and poetry from a merry heart which doeth good like a medicine. (Proverbs 17:22) I hope that I inspire you along the way. Enjoy the journey (again) with me.

I Do Know Something

I'll be fine in my knowing – eventually.

I have a friend who calls me every day. The same two questions are always asked: "How are you today?" And "What do you know?" I always answer. "I'm fine," and "Nothing."

But then, I think I'm 60 plus years old. I'm in the winter of my life. I do know something. In fact, I know a lot of stuff. It's all a glob in my head like the fat that comes to the surface when you make chicken soup. It doesn't taste so good until you stir it a little bit and mix that fat into the broth. I think what I know about life is a lot like chicken soup – thoughts aren't much good if they're not stirred occasionally. So the next time my friend calls, and asks me, "How are you?" I'll probably still say "fine." No doubt we'll chat a little bit, just like we always do, as we've done for the past ten years. But when asked as we're chatting, "So, what else do you know?" I'm going to say, "I do know something, in fact, I know a lot!"

I know I am much happier when I am serving God and walking the path He wants me to walk. You cannot walk someone else's path, live another's dream—you won't be happy. When you get off the path, the road can get a little bumpy.

I know that "…God will make known to me the path of life…" Psalm 16:11. I believe that to be true. I believe that God knows my steps before I take them. If He were not guiding my steps, lighting my path, I'd have gone over the cliff years ago. In fact, some days I am over the cliff, but thankfully, He's holding my hand and never leaves me hanging too long.

I know that He cares about me and that He knows every hair

on my head. When you stop to think about it, that's really something worth knowing.

I know I am special in God's eyes, unique in my creation. There is nobody on the face of this earth quite like me – Thank God for that. Two of me would be more than the world could take. If you don't believe me just ask my friends!

I know I belong to God. You must take confidence in knowing where you belong.

I also know my God-given talent is to write. Writing makes me happy and gives me a sense of completeness. It took me a long time to realize that it doesn't matter if I ever publish another book, or if anyone reads this book; writing gives me a sense of purpose and maybe that's all God meant for it to do.

I know that I personally need to make some changes in my life. Making a resolution to change something is a nice thought, but we have to do more than think about it. If you have an unhappy situation in your life, if you're going through something you don't like – if you're thinking "life stinks" then do something to change it. Don't let "stinking thinking" control your every moment. Life is a beautiful, wonderful gift from God. What we do with our lives is our gift to Him. Make every moment count.

I know that I need to read the Word and pray more. Prayer doesn't really change things – it changes people and people change things. But mostly, I need to get back on the path that God had me walking and that may mean letting go of some things and some people in my life. Letting go and letting God take control. I think it means I'm climbing back into the rowboat. That's what I know for now.

"We ought to act with God in the greatest simplicity, speaking to him frankly, plainly and imploring His assistance in our affairs, just as they happen." —Brother Lawrence.

Something else I know. Never sail through life in a rowboat without God!

How to Be Happy Without Really Trying

Being happy isn't that hard.

January 14, 2007, pastor's brother, John, was the guest speaker at church. He's a very good preacher, but just in case Pastor might actually read these words someday, I want him to know I still appreciate his teachings. Getting back to Pastor John…he spoke on, "Happiness." I know he was speaking from a spiritual point of view, but still, I find "happiness" an interesting subject. I've been searching for the meaning of true happiness most of my life.

What I learned about being happy without really trying is… although it sure helps to make one's life more comfortable, money doesn't make anyone happy. I know that when you die you can't take it with you. You come in into this world without anything and you leave the same way. My husband doesn't make me happy. And you know what? I shouldn't expect him to make me happy, it's not his job. Do my friends make me happy? Sometimes, maybe. I'll talk about what I learned about friendship, later. Back to happiness…I like to study people, watch them interact. I don't see a lot of happy going on. I see people going through the motions of trying to be "happy" but nothing seems real. I think this is an unhappy world and that as a people we have a lot to worry about.

When I was kid growing up in the 40s and 50s, we didn't have to worry about terrorist attacks and drive-by shootings. No one was badgering the courts to take God out of the schools. We could read our Bibles anywhere and anytime we wanted. We didn't have to worry about being politically correct. We just had to worry about obeying our parents and respecting our elders. Things have changed. In our concerns just to survive, it easy to forget how to be happy.

A lot of great people had a lot of 'great' things to say about happiness:

Mark Twain said, "Happiness is a Swedish sunset—it is there for all, but most of us look the other way and lose it."

Anatole France said of happiness, "…it is what we do not know."

Every once in awhile we see a headline in the newspaper: *The Secret of Happiness.* According to E.W. Howe, there is no such secret.

"Happiness and beauty are by-products. Folly is the direct pursuit of happiness and beauty." Says George Bernard Shaw.

Kin Hubbard, said, "It's pretty hard to tell what does bring true happiness: poverty and wealth have both failed."

Pastor John says true happiness comes from serving God with all of your heart, mind and soul -- your whole being. I suppose he's right. Happiness should start with knowing God, but it doesn't always happen that way.

This is what I've learned about happiness…each of us has to dig way down, deep into the very depths of our soul to figure out what makes us happy. Writing used to make me happy….I guess in a general sense it still does, when I make time to do it. You see, that's the thing about life – we get so busy living life to its fullest that happy gets lost and we forget what it is and what it feels like. Maybe we'd actually find happiness if we'd quit searching so hard for it; it's probably right in front of our noses.

> "I found a little remedy to ease the life we live and make each day a "happy" one – it is the word forgive. Happiness is possible only when one is busy. The body must toil, the mind must be occupied, and the heart must be satisfied. Those who do good as opportunity offers are sowing seed, and need not doubt the harvest."
> —From the book *Apples of Gold.*

You want to be happy, think positive, happy thoughts and you'll be happy

What I Know About Courage...

I learned from my mother.

I know that my mother was a woman of courage. I was born in the forty's, a post-war, out of wedlock baby. I was told my mother struggled with the decision to keep me or give me up for adoption. She chose to keep me and that took courage, especially since I was born with cerebral palsy. She had to know it would not be an easy life raising a handicap child alone.

Even though she may not have said it enough, I know that my mother loved me because she told me so and I believed her.

Growing up in the 40s and 50s was not easy. There was no such thing as "physically challenged." I was the crippled kid and it took courage just to survive that. I know that I got that courage from my mother. She always told me, "There is nothing you can't do if you put your mind to it."

My mother married my father when I was three years old. I grew up on a farm six and a half miles north of Reese, Michigan. I knew as a kid growing up that courage would guide me through life. I didn't learn to ride a bike until I was almost 11 and the first time I rode it, I went into the ditch, tore my dress and ruined my first pair of black paten-leather shoes! I took that courage my mother gave me and got right back on that bike determined that I would master it and I did. While other kids were out playing baseball, running, jumping, skipping, I was in my room writing short stories and poetry.

In spite of the fact that my 10th grade English teacher told me I'd never amount to much and that I would never be a writer because I couldn't spell, I always knew that I would grow up and be a writer, if for no other reason than to spite Mrs. Baker. I knew this because in my heart I was already a writer. I graduated from Reese High School, Northeastern School of Commerce Business College and Delta College with one goal in mind to courageously step out and be the writer I knew God created me to be.

I tried milking a cow, riding a horse and going to beauty school – none of which worked for me. The cow knocked me off the milking stool. I fell off the horse twice. And, I was a beauty school drop out. I didn't like putting my hands in gobs of hair gel. And besides, to be a beautician means standing on your feet all day. There were days I could hardly walk. What was I thinking?

I wanted to be the next great American novelist, but I settled for a career as a billing clerk in a medical office. Until one day it dawned on me that I was off that God path again, out of the rowboat, so-to-speak. With all the courage I could muster, I resigned my job in the medical field (after nearly 19 years) and went back to college to be a writer. I was 38 years old standing in line to register for college with 18 year old, know-it-all high school seniors. I almost tripped over their book bags trying to get out of line, but courage wouldn't let me fail. "You can do all things through Christ who strengthens you." (Philippians 4:13)

Health problems over took me and I never got the four-year degree in journalism that I thought I needed in order to write a good book. I discovered that I didn't need a degree to write – what I needed was guts, determination – and courage. And, I had that! I did eventually become a writer. God saw to that. I worked as a freelance reporter for our local paper for over decade before I started my own Christian newspaper and eventually I ended up helping 27 other "wanna-be authors" publish their books. It's amazing what a little courage can do.

Some people see me as a pessimist walking around with a glass half empty; (I admit to being a whiner and complainer on occasion – often mistaken for pessimism) others think of me as more of an optimist with a half full glass. But the truth of the matter is – the glass is neither half empty nor half full. I entertain and make people laugh. I make them feel good—happy even; there's nothing pessimistic about that. I became a success because I simply thought of myself as courageous – thank you, Mother. By the way, in my book it doesn't matter if the glass is half empty or half full—it's what's inside that counts and my cup runneth over with blessings.

"Nothing but courage can guide life" —Vauvenargus

A great part of courage is doing what is necessary for you to do and, while you are doing it, remember that with Christ anything's possible!

"Leave something to wish for, so as not to be miserable from very happiness"
—*Baltasar Gracian*

What I know about Christmas...

I didn't learn from Santa.

"I have great confidence in the revelation that holidays bring forth."
—Benjamin Disrarli

Although I wear a sweatshirt that boldly says "Bah-hum-bug" on it. I actually love Christmas. I love the smell of it, the feel of it, and the joy of it. I look forward to it with great expectation. Except, Christmas 2003 felt different, somehow...

I woke early, just like I always do. The house was unusually quiet. Maybe it was because the kids weren't kids, anymore. Christmas doesn't hold the glitter of excitement that it does when you have kids. It changes when they grow up. It changes when you grow up.

But, in my mind, I still see little ones running down the hallway, shrieking with delight, "Santa has come!" My babies aren't babies any more. The meaning of Christmas has changed for them too, but they will have children of their own, someday, and perhaps, when they do, I will hear the shrieks of children running down the hall once again. Oddly, in memories, Christmas stays the same for parents; at least it has for me.

Fumbling with the stereo button, careful to keep the music low, I turned on the Christmas lights, just like I have done every year since I can remember. I settled myself in the burgundy recliner, the one we bought for my mother-in-law, when she began having difficulty getting in and out of a chair. What I know now that

I wish I didn't know is that I need that chair just as much, if not more than my mother-in-law did.

I sat that year, Christmas 2003, watching the lights on the Christmas tree blink on and off, staring intently at the angel gracing the treetop. My daughter had put it there only days ago. I thought to myself, *if I stare long enough and hard enough, Mattie 3, and Heidi 6, would come bouncing down the hall, leap into my arms and shout into my ear, "It's Christmas!" clapping their hands with glee, eager to tear into the mounds of gifts piled beneath the tree.*

Not so this particular Christmas as I sat in reflection of days past. I knew then just like I know now Christmas at the Hawkins house will not be like that Christmas when Heidi was 6 and Matthew was 3 ever again. Instead of waiting for bounding children, I sat quietly in the chair watching through the window -- wet snow falling. Some people's prayers were answered – it would be a white Christmas after all. I sat as I do every Christmas, pondering about the days of my life… happy times – and some not so happy. More not so happy, lately. I suppose unhappy can be attributed to the fact that I am entering the winter of my life. What I know that I wish I didn't know is that aging will not be an easy time for me. Most people embrace it – not me. I am dreading it because I know that with aging comes less mobility, at least for me. I can't change it. I can't ignore it. I can't fight it. It's a fact, plain and simple…ah, remember, courage.

My eyes darted to the manger proudly displayed on top of the TV console. My winter thoughts of life, for the moment anyway, forgotten. I lovingly held the figurine of the baby Jesus in my hands…thinking about his life and his death. The pain he must have endured as he entered the winter of his life.

2003 had been an incredibly long year; one filled with trial and temptations—hurts and heartache – and love to bring healing.

I know I don't have such a bad life, I think this to myself. In fact, life is good because God is good to me. Feeling the beginning of a shiver. I pulled the afghan my mother had made me years ago around my chilled body…last year at this time I was in the hospital with a stress induced asthma attack, not sure if I'd be home for Christmas…

On Christmas Eve with the smell of home baked cookies and pies dancing through my head I told my doctor I had to go home. I could not picture myself missing Christmas Eve service at church, a tradition in our family that could not be missed. No way—not for me. It had been a trying year and I needed to end it on a positive note.

And what does this have to do with what I know about Christmas? Everything. Like Disrrarli, I also have great confidence in the revelation that holidays, especially Christmas, bring forth – and that revelation is love. I think love is the answer to all the world's problems. If men would stop fighting one another long enough to realize the value of love, it would be a lovely world.

I know that we need a little bit of Christmas and the revelation it brings all year long – that's what I know about Christmas!

"Wit is the rarest quality to be met with among people of education, and the most common among the uneducated."
— *William Hazlett*

Positive Thoughts…

Come from "positively" knowing God.

Lately, I've been starting my morning watching Joyce Meyer's program on joyful living. It makes for a rather amazing start to my day. It helps me to think about my life and what I'm doing or not doing. Life is truly amazing. It's the "maze" part of it that has me baffled sometimes. We human are just like those experimental laboratory mice, running through all those little mazes before we finally figure out where we are going.

Life is so simple yet we make it so complicated. Most of the complicated part comes from negative thinking. If you start your day with negative thoughts you can be assured the rest of your day will go wrong. My mother once told me that I needed to change my attitude, that everything I do or say affects somebody, somewhere. My family, my friends, even my spirituality are touched by the power of my thoughts. I can choose what and how I want to think, whether or not I want to be happy or sad.

The new hype is a book called *The Secret*. I happened to turn on the TV one day and saw Dr. Michael Beckwith and James Arthur Ray reviewing this book. It's a new age book, however, its focus – the power of positive thinking isn't anything new. It's in the Bible, "Be transformed by the renewing of your mind…" (Romans 12:2). "All things are possible in Christ…" (Matthew 19:20). "Consider it a joy my breathen when you encounter various trials for trails produce endurance and character…" (James 1:12). "He cares about you…" (I Peter 5:7). God promises to meet all of our needs. He will never leave us. How more positive can you get?

The Secret talks about the law of attraction, how a negative attitude attracts negative people with negative dispositions. My mother told me that when I was six!

My former pastor spoke one time on how your attitude determines your altitude (your relationship with God). The power of positive thinking isn't new to me. I've heard about it, talked about it, read about. I just seem to have trouble living it.

I wanted to write the author of this new age book and say, "Hey, you're not spouting anything new. It's in God's book."

I was reading a romance magazine one time -- I was about twelve -- my mother pulled it right out of my hands and threw it in the trash. "What did you do that for?" I complained.

"Because that's not something a 12-year old needs to be reading," she said. End of discussion.

As Christians we have to be careful of what we read, see, hear – and think. Joyce Meyer says in many of her books --learn to think for yourself. THINK about what you are doing and the consequences of your actions. Don't let other people do your thinking. Sounds like positive instruction to me.

The Secret also talked about leading negative lives gives off negative energy, which causes depression and fatigue, self doubt, unbelief and a multitude of other non-spiritual lifestyles. And that sometimes what we think about ourselves creates negative energy. Dr. Vincent Peale wrote about that in his book, "The Power of Positive Thinking." Dr. Wayne Dryer wrote about it, and Dr. Phil is writing about it! Some would say new age material is bad. I say, God created everything. He gave us a mind to THINK with. There are lots of books out there that may not be written from the Christian point of view. Still, you can learn some very valuable lessons from these books. You just have to think their philosophies through.

The Bible is quick to point out that the mind is a powerful thing, if only we as Christians would realize the power we have in Christ and that we need to learn how to pray believing we'll receive something from God. We should go through life anticipating that something good will happen and be participants of the goodness of life. Focus on NEW things. We are new creations in Christ.

I am a worrier. Sadly, I have passed this bothersome trait unto my son. My social worker daughter is more like her father. Forget the old, the past is history, it's over. Move on. Choose your battles; worry about important things. That's what she's always telling me. I hate to admit it, but she is right. The future hasn't happened yet. All we have is now – today. God's gift to us is life. What we do with that life is our gift to God. I think we need to focus our attention on gratitude, taking action to move forward.

Stop trying so hard to live the good life – just do it. Let God worry about your fears and inadequacies. Mom had a theory, and used it a lot. I used to say…I want this or that, or maybe this or that could happen. I'll ask God about it. When God didn't give me what I wanted, I was all bummed out. My mother would tell me, "Sometimes you got to help God. What's Connie doing?" Those words still ring true today, at least for me. Praying is good. We should all pray, every day. But might I suggest that we help God out a little by doing our part. *The Secret* suggests that you make a list of everything you don't want and then see what you can do about changing things. For some odd reason this makes sense to me, probably because I am a list maker. I make lists for everything. (Once you turn 50 – you have to do that – or you forget things!)

I don't have to think twice about my list. I pretty much know what I "don't" want.

1) I don't want to be fat
2) I don't want to live without financial security
3) I don't want an unhappy marriage
4) I don't want to live my life being sick all the time
5) I don't want to hang out with negative people
6) I don't want to procrastinate about doing more writing

If you're going to make an "I don't want list" then you also need to make an exact opposite list. What do you want and how can you get it?

This list was obviously going to be a little more difficult for me. I have no clue what I'm supposed to be doing about any of these things.

"Yes, you do." Mother again! If she were here she'd sit right down and write me a letter, help me with the "How I can help God to achieve my goals" list. How hard can this be?

1) I can make a conscious effort to lose weight, not just in my head but with my whole being -- heart, body and soul. Gee, I thought I did that. I joined Weight Watchers.

"How can anybody spend over $500 and be in Weight Watchers two years and still weigh the same as when you started?" My doctor wanted to know.

"It's the scales! We need universal scales."

Truth: I was trying to be in control, even when I was out of control. I can let God be in control of my lack of self-control. Or, I can take the easy way out and simply learn to love myself the way that I am, look at myself through God eyes and know that I am His perfect creation.

2) I want financial security. Who wouldn't? I'm not too old to get a part time job. Well, maybe not a job. But, I can stop spending money foolishly. I can pay off my credit card bills. I can learn to be content to live a more simple life. I need to realize that my security lies in Jesus Christ, my Provider, my Counselor and Wonderful Friend who will meet all of my needs—not K-Mart.

3) I want a happy marriage. Joyce Meyer said if you're unhappy about something, if something isn't working -- FIX it! That sounds simple enough. The question is how do I do that? After all, most of the problems in my marriage are not my fault.

"Wrong." Is that you, Mother?

OK, I could turn the problems and trails I face in every day life over to God. I have to stop being one of those people who lay my burdens at the cross and then pick them up again. Let go and let God--this means trusting Him to know what's best for me.

I think what I want most in my life is peace, the kind of peace that surpasses all understanding. His peace. I'm not sure how to go about it, but I have a feeling it begins with forgiveness (and that includes forgiving myself), and letting go of bitterness and anger. Peace comes in making a conscious effort to make changes in whatever phase of life is causing you stress. Stress, resentment, bitterness, and worry are not friends of peace nor are they friends of God. God says, "Don't be anxious about anything…" (Philippians 4:6) Mom can't claim that one!

You know you can make sense out of your life not by reading self-help books, although no doubt they can be helpful, but by reading The Bible, focusing on God's Word. He always has a word just for you. His grace is sufficient. Everything you need to know about life is in His book. There's an answer for every question. You don't need a self-help book to tell you what you need to know. You just need to know what truth is and that the truth shall set you free. And what's true about forgiveness is that it releases a great sense of relief. The truth about change is that it's good for you. Change me Lord; make me into your image. Make the wrongs in your life right – it'll liberate you and give you the courage you need to face your realities. God hates whiners and complainers so work on developing a positive attitude. We really are a blessed people. Instead of counting your problems, try counting your blessings. You'll be surprised at what the Lord has done in your life. Peace is yours for the asking. Affirmative thinking brings right actions. Find your path, your direction. Allow God to be in control of where you're going. If you're going to sail through life in a rowboat, isn't it easier if someone is in the boat with you? How about letting that someone be God?

Life is not met to be a struggle; it's met to be joyfully abundant. You will never have peace until you have peace with yourself and peace with God. God is in us. We are in God. Maybe you just have to write God a letter....Dear God; I'm lost please come and find me!

"If man had wished for what it is right, he might have had it a long time ago." —William Hazelitt

If we'd spend more time on our knees we might actually get some answers!

"An ounce of work is worth many pounds of 'words."
— *Sr. Francis DeSales*

Prayer Doesn't Have To Be Difficult

It's actually quite simple.

I've never had difficulty praying. My difficulty comes from believing in what I'm praying about. Have you ever had trouble talking to God? Have you struggled, wondering what to do? What to say? Have you thought about an empty chair? Picturing Jesus sitting across from you? It works. I've tried it. Now, when I talk to Jesus, I picture him sitting across from me, next to me, in the car with me, in the same room with me.

Of course, some of my friends think I'm a little weird (I prefer the word "unique".) They see me talking to myself sometimes, but that's OK, because I know who I'm talking too!

The neat thing about prayer is, if you stop talking long enough to listen to God, He might actually answer your prayers. The following (based on a true story) might help.

Sara's father was dying; she asked the minister to come and pray with her father, thinking it might help ease his pain and give him a sense of peace. When the minister arrived, he found the man lying in bed with his head propped up on two pillows. An empty chair sat at his bedside.

"I guess you were expecting me," said the minister.

"Not really, who are you?" The man asked.

"I'm Rev. Davis. You're daughter asked me to come and pray with you. I saw the empty chair and I figured you knew I was going to show up,"

"Oh, the chair," said the bedridden man, "that's for Jesus."

The minister looked puzzled for a minute.

"I have never told anyone this, not even my daughter," said the man. "But all of my life I have never known how to pray. At church I used to hear the pastor talk about prayer, but it went right over my head. I abandoned any attempt at prayer," the old man continued, "until one day four years ago; my best friend said to me, John, prayer is just a simple matter of having a conversation with Jesus. Here is what I suggest. Sit down in a chair; place an empty chair in front of you, and in faith see Jesus on the chair. It's not spooky because he promised;' I will be with you always'. Then just talk to him in the same way you're doing with me right now.'"

"So, I tried it and I've liked it so much that I do it a couple of hours every day."

"That's great!" Rev. Davis smiled.

"I'm careful though. If my daughter saw me talking to an empty chair, she'd either have a nervous breakdown or send me off to the funny farm." The old man chuckled. "Me and Jesus." He gave the minister thumbs up.

The minister was deeply moved by the man's story and encouraged the old man to continue on his faith journey. Then he prayed with him, anointed him with oil, and returned to the church.

Two nights later the man's daughter called to tell the Rev. Davis that her daddy had died that afternoon.

"Did he die in peace?" Davis asked.

"Yes, when I left the house about two o'clock, he called me over to his bedside, told me he loved me and kissed me on the cheek. When I got back from the store an hour later, I found him dead. But there was something strange about his death. Apparently, just before Daddy died, he leaned over and rested his head on the chair beside the bed. What do you make of that?" The daughter asked.

The minister wiped a tear from his eye and said, "I wish we could all go like that talking to the empty chair."

Prayer is one of the best free gifts we receive. If you're not talking to Jesus everyday, maybe it's time to start. Get Him a chair!

(This story first appeared in Connie's Corner – His Banner Newspaper, February of 2007)

Stop Making Resolutions

They don't work.

I am an avid resolution maker and breaker; I admit it. Even so, I think of each New Year as a time to make changes – call them resolutions if you'd like. I prefer to call them lifestyle changes. You don't need to wait for the dawn of a New Year to think about making changes. I'm like a chameleon, constantly changing…my looks, my hairstyle, my outfits, sometimes even my persona changes. I confuse my family and friends daily.

"Who is Mother today?" is the question my kids asked one another.

"I don't know," my husband answers, "but I'm never bored."

One year for my birthday I went out and bought a wig. My friend bet me $5 that my husband would notice immediately. I know my husband. I was pretty sure he wouldn't notice immediately or otherwise.

I played it up big time, walking into the kitchen flinging my new shoulder-length dark brown locks. "So, how was your day?" I asked.

"Fine," he said. He was on the phone so I guess I shouldn't have really expected him to notice me.

Men are not known for being multi-tasked. Most can only think about one thing at a time and as I entered the kitchen he was thinking about his phone conversation. Not only did I have fun creating a personality (Amada Cooper) to go along with the wig. I won $5 from my friend! (I'll talk about Amanda Cooper later, maybe.)

When he finally did notice, and as I was explaining to him that he wasn't going to be happy; I spent $150 on a wig and it wasn't even human hair. He started to laugh. I wasn't sure he was laughing at me or with me. "That's OK," he chuckled. "I just bought a snow blade for my tractor and it cost a whole lot more than a wig!"

OK then, change is good!

Change can be difficult, but not impossible. I think the big thing about change is that it takes us down a new path, away from our comfort zone, but in essence, change can also bring us closer to God, in tune to the life he wants for us. There was a chorus that we used to sing back in the 80s, "Lord change me into your image…" Sometimes to get where He wants us to be, involves allowing Him to change us into His image. Whether we want to admit it or not, change is good for us!

Some people feel that any great and sudden change is death. The Bible talks a lot about dying to our sins. When we decide to follow Jesus we die to self, our old nature. We become a new creation in Christ. In that respect a great and sudden change is good.

"We must always change, renew, rejuvenate ourselves; otherwise we harden." A quote from Goethe. An interesting quote that one should seriously take to heart. To be more Christ-like should be number one on our resolution list for any New Year—to live a godly life; to be kind, gentle, meek, humble, cheerful, and helpful. In order to do that, we need to be willing to let go of the things that keep us from achieving great spiritual heights and then strive to be ambassadors for Christ. Our prayer should always be, "Father, change us into Your image" and then to be ready to be molded and reshaped into exactly what God wants for us!

(*From Connie's Corner – His Banner Newspaper, January 2007*)

What Ever Happened to Common Sense?

The older I get the more I am amazed by the lack of common sense in mankind. I laugh myself silly over some of the not so bright things we humans do and wonder if God is having a good laugh, too? Or maybe, He's just plain sad. Sometimes, I find myself wondering if God is asking Himself, "Whatever happened to common sense?"

My mother used to say, "We don't use the brains God gave us." Simple things, like knowing when to come in out of the rain; why the early bird gets the worm, or that life isn't always fair and maybe it was my fault (we certainly have a hard time admitting to that last one). The simple things in life, knowing right from wrong, treating others the way we would like to be treated are just common sense, things we are supposed to learn as we live life. Behavior God expects from us. It makes you kind of wonder whatever happened to common sense, anyway. Considering the state our country is in, it wouldn't surprise me if common sense is dead. I bet the obituary would read something like this:

Obituary of the late Common Sense

Today we mourn the passing of a beloved old friend, Common Sense, who has been with us for many years. No one knows for sure how old he was, since his birth records were lost in bureaucratic red tape long ago. He will be remembered as having cultivated such valuable lessons as: living by simple, sound financial policies (don't spend more than you can earn) and reliable strategies (adults, not children, are in charge). I bet that's one young people haven't heard. Common Sense's health began to deteriorate rapidly when well-intentioned but overbearing regulations were set in place. Reports of a six-year-old boy charged with sexual harassment for kissing a classmate; teens suspended from school for using mouthwash after lunch; and a teacher fired for reprimanding an unruly student, only worsened his condition.

Common Sense lost ground when parents attacked teachers for doing the job that they themselves had failed to do in disciplining their unruly children. It declined even further when schools were required to get parental consent to administer, sun lotion or a band-aid to a student, but could not inform parents when a student became pregnant and wanted to have an abortion. Does this make sense?

Common Sense lost the will to live as the Ten Commandments became contraband; when God was taken out of schools; when churches became businesses; and criminals received better treatment than their victims. Common Sense took a beating when you couldn't defend yourself from a burglar in your own home and the burglar could sue you for assault. Common Sense finally gave up the will to live, after a woman failed to realize that a steaming cup of coffee was hot. She spilled a little in her lap, and was promptly awarded a huge settlement for her stupidity. (How stupid is that?) The world became sue happy.

Sadly, Common Sense was preceded in death by his parents, Truth and Trust, his wife, Discretion, his daughter, Responsibility, and his son, Reason. He is survived by his three stepbrothers: I Know My Rights, Someone Else Is To Blame, and I am a Victim.

When Common Sense died not many attended his funeral because few realized he was gone! If that's you, shame on you. If that's me, God help me to change and stand up for Truth, Trust, Discretion, Responsibility, Reason – and most of all, Common Sense!

(Thanks to my Internet friends for helping me with this article. This article first appeared in His Banner Newspaper, 2006.)

Sailing Through Life One Worry at a Time

Worry. Who me? The Bible tells us in Luke 12:29, that we should not worry, "Do not seek what you shall eat and what you shall drink, do not keep worrying." If contentment isn't a Fruit of the Sprit, it probably should be. If only we could learn the art of contentment.

When I think of all the "stupid" stuff I worry about and all the energy I put into it, I have to ask myself, "What am I thinking?" The problem is, I'm not thinking – I'm worrying!

My husband says I am a born worrier, that I should probably receive an award for "Best Worrier." He's right. I am a born worrier. It must be working because half the things I worry about never happen. I'm ready for that award now and will see that it finds a place of honor on the shelf with my other knickknacks to be admired and cherished. The Bible tells us over and over not to worry, not to be anxious about anything. Think of all the sleepless nights we spend worrying about one thing or another…all the burdens we insist on carrying, the joyless days and the restlessness that robs us of peace. Why is it when we know without doubt that Jesus is our comforter, that He bears all burdens, that we still insist on worrying our way through life? The joy of the Lord is our strength. The peace-destroying, love-destroying, happiness-destroying hours we waste on worry brings not one good thing into our lives.

Instead of spending time worrying over and about things that may never happen, maybe we should concentrate on things that give us joy, things that we know to be true. Something that truly satisfies us. The following was sent to me by one of my Internet friends. I think the words are worth sharing. Instead of worry it gives us something to think about – food for thought.

> The most useless thing to do is worry.
> The greatest joy in life is giving.
> The greatest loss is loss of self-respect.
> The most satisfying work you could ever do is to help others.
> The ugliest personality trait is selfishness.
> The greatest shot in the arm is encouragement.
> The greatest problem you'll ever over come is fear.
> The most effective sleeping pill you could ever take is peace of mind.
> The most powerful force in life is love.

So let's stop worrying about life and practice giving, helping others, working on self-esteem, being respectful of ourselves as well as others, being encouragers instead of whiners. There is no fear in the perfect love of God. A relationship with Him is peace of mind. If the world would just stop fighting long enough to practice the great commandment -- to love one another -- they would know the most powerful force in life, God's love.

I think if God can take care of the lilies of the field and the birds of the sky—he can certainly take care of we worry warts! Let's vow to STOP worrying. STOP being anxious and concentrate on seeking the things of the Kingdom. For where your treasure is there will your heart be also. (Matthew 6:21)

> *"We can always get along better by reason and love of truth than by worry of conscience and remorse. Harmful are these and evil, inasmuch as they form a particular kind of sadness; and the disadvantages of sadness I have already proved and shown that we should strive to keep these things, worry, remorse, evil and sadness from our lives."*
> —Spinoza (paraphrased).

> *"Happy is the man who has broken the chains, which hurt the mind, and given up worrying once and for all."* —Ovid

The worse thing we can do is worry about what we should of, could of or didn't do with our lives. We need to learn to be content in whatever phase of life we are in. Now, where did I put that instruction book on contentment, again?

My Mind Is In A Muddle

Why is that?

Muddle: Def. To bring into disorder, bewildered, confused. Muddle: late Middle English, perhaps from Middle Dutch, derived from "modden", which means to "dabble in mud." Confused was initially associated with alcoholic drink (late 17th century), giving rise to 'busy oneself' in a confused way and "rumble up." (19th century) (From the Oxford American Dictionary.)

There are days when I feel as if I just can't function. Days that I feel as if I'm going nowhere fast, totally confused; my mind is in a muddle, unsure of what to do, what path to follow. I am in a definite state of rumbling up. I'm sure I'm not the only Christian who has felt this way. We pray. We look to God for answers, but none seem to come forth and suddenly we find ourselves stuck in a rut, dabbling in mud; our minds in a muddle, a state of confusion, wondering what to do next.

I believe that God has a plan for each an every one of his children. The Bible says, "…our paths are set before us…" (Psalm 16:11) In my *Sailing Through Life In A Rowboat* book, you will notice a rowboat on the cover; there are no oars. I always tell people when I speak about that book there are no oars because God controls the direction in which I should go. The problem is, we are an impatient people and we want to know where we are going and when we will arrive. Sometimes, we are already where God wants us; we just don't know it.

So next time you think of yourself as "stuck in a rut" when

your mind is muddled, or you find yourself wallowing in the mud, take time to talk to God, listen to His still small voice. Look at the beautiful day He has given you. If you got up this morning on your own, you're doing well. Begin your day with joy in your heart, keeping in mind, this is the day that the Lord has made we should be glad and rejoice in it. Trust Him to take you where He wants you to go even if He takes you there in a little red rented rowboat!

The First Day of School is Wonderful!

Especially if you're a mother.

I thought this article that came to me via of the Internet was a perfect back to school story for this book. It's about goodness and mercy. Even though my children are grown it made me smile, remembering those good old golden rule days, the last day of summer and the first day of going back to school! If you're a mother, then you've no doubt experienced the following story yourself.

A young mother was concerned about her kindergarten son walking to school. Timmy didn't want his mother to walk with him; after all, he was a big boy now. She wanted to give him the feeling that he had some independence but yet know that he was safe.

She had an idea. She asked her neighbor, Mrs. Goodnest, if she would please follow Timmy to school in the mornings, staying at a distance so he wouldn't notice her. Mrs. Goodnest said that since she was up early with her toddler anyway, it would be a good way for them to get some exercise as well so she agreed to the plan

The next school day, Mrs. Goodnest and her little girl, Marcy, set out following behind Timmy as he walked to school with another neighbor boy. The neighbor faithfully followed Timmy and his friend for the whole week.

As the boys walked and chatted, kicking stones and twigs, Timmy's little friend noticed the same lady was following them as she seemed to do every day all week. Finally he said to Timmy, "Have you noticed that lady following us to school all week? Do you know her?"

Timmy nonchalantly replied, "Yeah, I know who she is".

"Well, who is she"? Timmy's friend asked.

"Oh, that's just Shirley Goodnest", Timmy replied, "and her daughter Marcy".

"Shirley Goodnest? Who's she and why is she following us"?

"Well", Timmy explained, "every night my mom makes me say the 23rd Psalm, 'cuz she worries about me, it says, 'Shirley Goodnest and Marcy shall follow me all the days of my life', so I guess I'll just have to get used to it."

Now in closing, may the Lord bless you and keep you; may the Lord make his face to shine upon you, and be gracious to you; may the Lord lift His countenance upon you, and give you peace. (Numbers 6:22-26) and may Shirley Goodnest and Marcy be with you always!

(This article first appeared in The Crossroads Newspaper, 2004.)

A Telephone Call to God

Wouldn't that be cool?

With all the hype Valentine's Day gets, it's easy when you have no special Valentine in your life to get depressed about all this "love" stuff. But truly there is someone who will always love you no matter what. His name is Jesus. If you need a friend, He's there. Have you ever wondered what a telephone call to God might be like? I have…I've played it out a million times in my mind.

    Hello God. I called tonight to talk a little while. I need a friend who'll listen to my anxiety and trials. You see, I can't quite make it through a day just on my own… I need your love to guide me so I'll never feel alone, especially on Valentine's Day. You see, I don't have a special Valentine in my life. So, will you be my Valentine? I knew that you would.

    While I'm on the phone, I want to ask you please to keep my family safe. Come and fill their lives with confidence for whatever fate they're bound. And give me faith, dear God, to face each hour throughout the day, and not to worry over things I can't change in any way. It helps to remind me that worry adds not one single day to my life.

    I thank you God for being home and listening to my call, for giving me such good advice when I stumble and fall. Your number, God, is the only one that answers every time. I never get a busy signal, never had to pay a dime! And I can always count on you to be the perfect Valentine.

    So thank you, God, for listening to my troubles and my sorrows. Good night, God. What's that? You love me. I love you, too. I'll call again tomorrow, I promise.

Wouldn't it be awesome if there were a phone line to God or a post office in heaven so your loved ones who have gone home could write? You don't have to call God on the telephone to have this conversation; He's available to talk to you anytime. In fact, He's waiting to hear from you now. God bless you!

Don't Let One of God's Bricks Hit You in the Head...

It hurts!

I can't take credit for the following story, but after reading it, I know for sure, I don't want to get hit in the head by one of God's bricks – it hurts! Maybe it's time to listen to what God has to say.

A young and successful executive was traveling down a neighborhood street, going a bit too fast in his new Jaguar. He was watching for kids darting out from between parked cars and slowed down when he thought he saw something.

As his car passed, no children appeared. Instead, a brick smashed into the Jag's side door! He slammed on the brakes and backed the Jag back to the spot where the brick had been thrown. The angry driver then jumped out of the car, grabbed the nearest kid and pushed him up against a parked car shouting, "What was that all about and who are you? Just what the heck are you doing? That's a new car and that brick you threw is going to cost a lot of money. Why did you do it?"

The young boy was apologetic. "Please, mister, please, I'm sorry but I didn't know what else to do," he pleaded. "I threw the brick because no one else would stop." With tears dripping down his face and off his chin, the youth pointed to a spot just around a parked car. "It's my brother." He said "He rolled off the curb and fell out of his wheelchair and I can't lift him up." Now sobbing, the boy asked the stunned executive, "Would you please help me get him back into his wheelchair? He's hurt and he's too heavy for me."

Moved beyond words, the driver tried to swallow the rapidly swelling lump in his throat. He hurriedly lifted the handicapped boy back into the wheelchair, then took out a linen handkerchief and dabbed at the fresh scrapes and cuts. A quick look told him everything was going to be okay.

"Thank you and may God bless you," the grateful child told the stranger.

Too shook up for words, the man simply watched the boy push his wheelchair-bound brother down the sidewalk toward their home. It was a long, slow walk back to the Jaguar. The damage was very noticeable, but the driver never bothered to repair the dented side door. He kept the dent there to remind him of this message: "Don't go through life so fast that someone has to throw a brick at you to get your attention!"

God whispers in our souls and speaks to our hearts. Sometimes when we don't have time to listen, He has to throw a brick at us. It's our choice to listen or not.

(This article first appeared in His Banner Newspaper, 2007.)

What Constitutes a Good Friend?

I like that old saying, "A stranger is just a friend you haven't met yet." I don't know who said it, but I like it and I have tried over the years to apply that principle of friendship in my life. There are no strangers in my life, only friends.

Some friends come into your lives and quickly go. Some friends stay awhile, touch your heart and are gone. I have friends who have come into my life, to sit and chat, and hold my hand. Friends who laugh with me and cry with me. Friends who have stayed longer than awhile, some forever. Each has touched my heart in a special way and I will never be the same because of their friendship.

The older I get the more I find myself thinking about life and the friendships I have made as I have sailed through life. None are so dear to my heart as my cousin, Marilyn, my oldest and dearest friend. (Not necessarily oldest in age).

We met when I was five and she was three. We have been good friends for over 50 years! Our friendship has lasted longer than some marriages!

We went through grade school together. She was the one who let me have the red crayon when all that was left was the ugly black one. She gave up her turn to ring the school bell and let me do it instead. It was my cousin Marilyn who helped me stand up to the bullies who teased me about the way I walked and shared lunch with me when I forgot mine.

During school dances she would always go up to Dickie Gilbert and tell him that I wanted to dance with him so I wouldn't be embarrassed. That's the kind of friend that Marilyn was. When we got in high school she saved me a seat on the bus and let me cut in line during lunch so I wouldn't have to stand so long on a bad leg. And she still defended me to the bullies and helped me face the giants in my life.

She helped me clean my brother's room. (Believe me that was an all day chore). There were scary things growing in that room and only a true friend would go there with me. We worked on scrapbooks together (long before there was such a thing as "scrap booking") and traded records of our favorite rock and roll singers, watched American Bandstand together and enjoyed the same sappy movies.

We shared secrets, laughter, tears, the thrill of getting our first job, first boyfriend and our first car. We mended broken hearts together.

She was there when my two children were born. She's been there through many trials and has shared my joy when those trials turned into triumphs. And I, hers.

Now that I am older (and hopefully wiser) my idea of a good friend hasn't changed. It is still the person who gives you the better of the two choices, holds your hand when you are scared, and helps you fight off those who try to take advantage of you. It's the person who thinks of you at times when you are not there, reminds you of what you have forgotten, helps you put the past behind you, but knows when you need to hold on just a little bit longer. One who stays with you so you have the confidence to do what you need to do, goes out of their way to make time for you, forgives you and helps you clear up your mistakes, clean up your act and still keeps on loving you.

A true friend helps you deal with the pressures in your life, smiles for you when you are sad, helps you to become a better person and most importantly loves you no matter what. Today, that is still my cousin, Marilyn. She is what I would call – a really good friend. A true friend. *(Modified, this article first appeared in The Crossroads Newspaper – April 2005, its final issue.)*

And now, I can thank God for a long list of friends throughout my life who have been there for me. Many have joined the ranks with Marilyn, honoring me by letting me call them "my" friends.

What I know about my friends sweeps me away. I can truly say I have a wonderful network of friends who are not only true, but loyal as well. They have certainly seen and heard the worst from me and still they call me "friend."

Friends that I can do nothing with and enjoy every single minute of it. I can't help but think of those times in my life that I simply enjoyed chatting on the phone. Betty and I could talk for hours, (we still can.) If we weren't on the phone we were on the computer just talking about everything, about nothing.

"What do you talk about all day long?" My husband wanted to know.

"Nothing in particular," I tell him. We just talk our way through life.

When I think about Lisa, Martha, Eva, Mary, Linda, Tarry, Sharron, Lorraine, Virginia, Donna, Jill, Darlan…the list goes on and on. It isn't the big things my friends do (or have done over the years) that stand out. It's the many little things they do that show me how much they care. Listening to the same stories over and over, putting up with my every day complaints, never forgetting a birthday or knowing just the right time to call and cheer me up. And hopefully I do the same for them.

I couldn't live without my friends. I wouldn't want to. I count on them more than family because it's been my friends who have been there with me in so many times of need. I cannot picture calling my brother at 1 AM in the morning with a problem, but I know I can always call Lisa. Lisa always calls me when she's walking (or jogging), it's our talk time. Better is a neighbor or a friend nearby than a brother who is far away.

George Washington said, "True friendship is a plant of slow growth." That's how my friendship with Julie began, a slow growth. A conversation here or there, lunch together, a phone call, sharing our stories of woe as well as our success stories. Little by little our friendship grew until one day she was riding the roller coaster of life with me, sailing in that rowboat, if you will, without an oar! Only a true friend would row without an oar.

Lots of people want to ride with you in your brand new Cadillac, but few when the car breaks down are willing to wait with you for the tow truck! Not too many friends will climb into a rowboat with you and trust you know where you're going or ride the ups and downs of life's roller coaster. Julie tells the best story of life in a rowboat. "I can't take it anymore," she said standing in the middle of my bedroom one day. You're up. You're down. You're in the boat. You're out of the boat. You're on the roller coaster, again. You're making me crazy, Girlfriend!" Julie is always willing to get in the boat and go crazy with me. That's a friend.

An anonymous author wrote: "*Love is blind; friendship closes its eyes."* That's Donald. He came into my life at a time when I was in great emotional turmoil. He didn't try to mold me or remake me. He simply closed his eyes to my faults and accepted me just as I was. In doing so, he helped me to see new ways of relating to life, new causes to consider. He was the first "male" friend I think I ever had. (I know there are those who think married women shouldn't have male friends and that men shouldn't have female soul mates, poppy cock.) I thank Donald, my friend, for helping me to see who I really am, for working with me in the publication of my first book. Without his encouraging words and strong push I would have never had the courage to explore new interests or to revisit the idea that I could be a published author. Together we started a successful publishing company, helping other authors to realize their dream to publish a book! Donald made the doldrums of my life more bearable at time when I needed new vision. We have sailed many rough waters together. We've had our ups and downs. It's been in the name of "friendship" that we have survived.

To all my friends (not just the afore mentioned), but to everyone who has called me "friend." I want to say: Thank you for being loyal to me, for supporting me in all my endeavors, even those that may have sounded crazy at the time, for keeping my secrets safe. I trust you all with my life and thank you for your willingness to be a part of my world and for letting me write about you in this book! Not only are my friends loyal, they are brave souls.

"Of all the things which wisdom provides to make life entirely happy, the greatest is the possession of friendships." —Epicurus

Voices of Influences

I hear voices when there's no one there.

To borrow a phrase from the popular children's television show Sesame Street, *"These are the people in my neighborhood...the people that I meet when I'm walking down the street...the people that I meet each day."*

I'm not writing about the people in my neighborhood in any particular order of importance, they're just people, family, friends, neighbors, acquaintances -- and even strangers (waiting to become friends) that have passed through my life. I guess you could say they are the voices of influence.

Lila

Aunt Lila (my mother's sister) was born Rose Lillian. She changed her name to Lillian Rose when she was 18, and then later in her life became "Lila". She is the person who most influenced my spiritual walk, praying for me from day one and I think has prayed for me daily since. She truly has been the person in my life "praying me through."

It was due to Lila's influence that I found Christ and accepted Him as my personal savior at the age of 13. I became a Bible-toting teenager, setting out on a great quest to know more about the love of Christ...to serve Him, to find out everything I could about Him. I guess you could say I fell in love with Jesus over and over again. That popular praise song of the 70s became my theme song.

As I grew older, my thirst for knowledge about a loving Savior also grew. I remember going to a home fellowship meeting in the early 80s listening to the people talk about how they came to know Christ. There were stories of wandering, soul searching, and torture as they came through unbelievable hardships to find the one that could save them and promise life eternal with Him. When it was my turn, I really didn't know what to say. I was lucky to have grown up in a Christian home. I went to church since—forever. I learned how to pray when I was a mere baby. I went to Sunday school, learned the Apostles Creed, the Lord's Prayer, and the Beatitudes. I grew up knowing about Jesus, so at 13 it was easy for me to walk down that isle at a youth rally, confess my sins and really give my heart to Christ, totally and completely. I didn't have sob stories, woeful stories or sad stories. I wasn't abused; I didn't have to go through rehab or detox in order to find Christ. He found me! And I accepted Him, thanks to the prayers of a righteous woman, my Aunt Lila.

Uncle Frank

I lived with my aunt and uncle until I was three and my mother married Willis and we went to live on the farm. He was building us a house. I slept in a youth bed under the dining room table until the house was finished and I moved upstairs. It was the first time I had a room of my own, but even so, I wasn't sure at that tender age if sleeping under the window in a youth bed or even having my own room was where I belonged. I was a city girl at heart. Willis became my dad a year later when I was four and he officially adopted me. I continued to live with my aunt and uncle (summers) until I was 13 and my uncle died. Uncle Frank in essence was my father figure. He was the man I went to when I was hurt, when some boy broke my heart…when I had questions about life. Two things I remember about Uncle Frank. He loved to sing. "*Cruising down the river on a Sunday afternoon…*" was one of his favorite tunes. On Saturday's we'd get up early and sneak down to Feather's Bakery on Columbus Avenue for sugar donuts. We'd take them to the park and eat them while we watched the boats cruise the river. He said some day he'd buy me a boat. He took me shopping for a new bike, new shoes and gave me money to buy ice cream at the local party store. We'd go to the amusement park and to see Tex Ritter in the movies. He'd loved a Sunday afternoon drive, pickled bologna, and fresh just-picked sweet corn and his dog, Mickey – and he loved me. I knew this without a doubt because he told me so and I believed him. As I grew up, we'd often sit and talk on the porch swing about life, and our dreams. I could share my secret wishes with Uncle Frank and trust him not to tell anyone.

"Connie," he told me, "don't give your heart away if you're not sure the man won't break it. And always be true to yourself." Boy, if I had only listened to that advice, I could have prevented heartaches by the number. I was devastated when my uncle died a few days before Christmas four months before my 13th birthday. I didn't have a chance to give him his Christmas present, nor the card I made him. I didn't get a chance to say, "Don't go, I love you."

Mrs. Baker

Mrs. Baker was my high school English teacher and not a very good one, I might add. She did not have a kind and loving spirit toward children. I wanted to be a writer more than anything in life. I tried as hard as I could to write things that I thought Mrs. Baker would like. I had a flare for the dramatic in my writing. She told me I was a terrible speller, that I couldn't put two sentences together, and that I'd never be a writer. In fact, she told me I probably wouldn't amount to anything. Not all voices of influence are positive. It was much later in life that I learned, creativity is equally as important to publishers. My head was full of creative ideas and many books were born from the spark of those ideas. In spite of the fact that I couldn't spell, I published six books!

I wonder what Mrs. Baker would think if she could see me now?

Peter Russell

Rev. Peter Russell was the pastor of the Munger Presbyterian Church in my youth. I can thank him for encouraging my public speaking abilities. As President of our youth group, I was often called upon to speak before my peers and before the church body. At least twice a year, we'd have "Youth Sunday", a special service lead by the youth of the church. I enjoyed the thrill of standing behind the podium, sharing my testimony of faith. Imagine years later, there I am Connie the author standing behind that very podium on that very stage sharing my life as an author and newspaper woman! Not only did our youth group participate in Sunday services, we did a radio show, too. Yes, I wrote some of the scripts that were used. Years later, I worked as a copywriter for a local radio station. Little did Rev. Russell know what a voice of influence he would turn out to be in my life.

Skip Renker

Mr. Renker taught Personal Journal Writing at Delta College. It was probably the best writing class I have ever taken. I have been an avid journal keeper since I was 11 years old, but those personal writing classes really inspired me to achieve my goal to become an author. Suddenly there was structure and purpose to my journaling. It was an intense class of personal life journey experiences; I learned to meditate on those experiences. I learned how to take what was inside my head and heart and put thoughts and feelings to paper. From the archives of my journal ideas for novels appeared. *Sailing Through Life In A Rowboat* was born from the pages of my journal. Many of the characters for my novels came out of my "people book" a journal about the interesting people I had met long life's way, or simply people I hadn't met that I thought were interesting in some way. Life's memories, special moments, and heartbreaks were all in the pages of spiral notebooks and later on my computer. My journal became my best friend, the one place where I could go and spend time with myself. It's where I learned to like myself; I think it's important to like yourself and become your own best friend. If you don't like yourself, it's hard to learn to like others and eventually love them.

If I were to meet Mr. Renker again, I'd tell him, "Thanks, because of your personal writing class," I went on to teach Creative Journaling Writing and Spiritual Journaling Workshops, using my journal as a tool to commune with God. Not only did I become an avid journal keeper, I taught my children the value of keeping a journal using their journal as a place to get in touch with their inner feelings.

Jimmy Felske

"*Jimmy Crack Corn and I don't care. Jimmy Crack Corn and I don't care...*" is the song my cousin, Marilyn, and I sang to our neighbor Jimmy Felske, brother to Larry and Dennis, son of Wilma and Walt. I had a crush on all three of the Felske boys. And why not, they were not only cute but endearingly kind. But the biggest crush was Jimmy Crack Corn. He was talk, dark and handsome. My cousin Marilyn still laughs thinking for years that Jimmy (who was away serving in the army most of our growing up years), was the hired hand. It seemed like the only time we saw him was in the barn working on a tractor or out in the field hoeing beans!

Jimmy was an accomplished musician who played the accordion, was in a polka band and later a country band. Believe it or not, he played at his own wedding reception. I loved to hear Jimmy play "*Lady of Spain.*" It was Mom's favorite song, too. I was thrilled when Jimmy showed me how to play the scales on his keyboard. I was hooked and begged my mother for an accordion of my own.

"Not until you learn how to play the piano," she said. What drudgery, but learn I did. I took piano lessons for two years from Rosemary Jay and was faithful to practice every day just so I could get an accordion. That day finally came. I don't remember exactly how old I was, ten, maybe twelve. I only know that Jimmy's cousin was selling his accordion (complete with music sheets) and my parents bought it for me! I was on cloud nine. I took lessons for seven years, was faithful to practice and played every day. Marilyn got an accordion a year later; she and I had instruction from the same lady and played in Dorothy's Accordion Band together. We spent many Saturday's learning the music to "Jimmy Crack Corn" and proudly played that song for Jimmy Felske.

The Felske's were a musical family. Walt played the Concertina and might have played the fiddle, too. I'm not sure if Larry played an instrument, but Dennis used to play the piano every morning in the one-room school we all attended. He mostly played by ear, but could he play the piano. I remember Saturday nights with the Felske's involved two things – music and playing Euchre!

Sometimes Dennis, Marilyn and I would make up songs. I was a member of the Glee Club in high school. I guess I thought that made me a singer. I remember standing in the stairway that lead up to my room with a hairbrush in my hand pretending to be Patsy Cline. I started writing songs on the piano as soon as I learned how to play. Later, I bought my own piano and made up fun, zippy kid songs for my children; songs like, *Raindrops falling on my sandbox*, and country songs for lost loves and praise songs for a savior I knew loved me even when I messed up. I was never very good at writing songs, but I did it anyway, because I enjoyed it, a talent I passed on to my son who some day will probably inherit the piano to go along with his guitars.

I finally learned how to play Euchre – Dennis would be proud and I still play the accordion! I still have a crush on Jimmy Felske and yes, he still plays the accordion!

On occasion I still write songs about lost loves and broken hearts. I still know the words to *Raindrops keep falling on my sandbox*. All is well in my musical world thanks to Jimmy Felske's voice of musical influence in my life.

Aunt Helen

If ever there was a teller of stories it was Aunt Helen (my dad's sister). This woman could spin a yarn—non-stop. She not only talked with her mouth but with her hands as well as her eyes. Very animated, she almost commanded attention to story-telling. She was a teacher and lived in Hazleton, Pennsylvania with her husband and five children. She wrote letters often telling stories of growing up on the farm, how she took the train to Detroit to visit her sisters. What it was like riding to church on Sunday's on the back of a hay wagon. It was from Aunt Helen's letters and the stories that she would tell that gave me a sense of family, the importance of history, knowing our ancestors and the contributions they made to our family.

My cousin Dan developed a great love of history from Aunt Helen and began to track the family tree until it became an eternal part of his life. My daughter Heidi who fell in love with the idea of scrap booking in college eventually make a family heritage album depicting life on both sides of our family "The Houghtaling's and The Hawkins." Pictures and stories seem to be the norm in our family – you can't do one without the other. It seemed natural that I would teach a memory making class combining the art of scrap booking and journal keeping.

We all get our talents from somewhere. I got my love of letter writing from Aunt Helen and my talent to tell a good story from both Helen and my mother – both of these women knew how to talk and in fact would try to out talk the other – it was almost a contest between them – who could talk the loudest, the longest and tell the best story. Now, that Mom and Aunt Helen are gone it's my turn to tell the stories!

"Storytelling is not an art, but more what we call a 'knack'."
—Sir Richard Steele

The Art of Telling a Good Story

Is to know a good story when you hear it.

As previously mentioned, I like my mother and my Aunt Helen, am a storyteller. My husband tells people my stories are mostly lies, "Seldom is any splendid story wholly true," says Samuel Johnson.

To set the record straight, I do not tell lies. I tell stories. I don't just make up stories for the fun of it. I tell stories to entertain, to make people feel good, to fill their mouths with laughter. There should be tellers of funny stories to visit the sick because laughter is good medicine.

It is now required of me that whenever I go to speak, I begin with a funny story, otherwise, I will surely be harassed which reminds me of the only time I was ever heckled. I was speaking to a group of ladies on a soggy Tuesday evening; the subject, my first dramatic work, *Journey to the Well*, a serious story about three men of God who embark on a journey to build a church and what happened to them when they lost their way. In the middle of my talk this little old lady jumps up, shakes her cane at me and says, "I didn't come here to hear woe-be-gone stories of people who lost their way. Where's the humor? Where's the laughter? Lets go sailing through life in a rowboat!"

All righty then. With that information and the image of being beat with a cane by a little old lady in my mind, I quickly closed the cover to "*Journey to The Well*", picked up a copy of "*Sailing Through Life...*" amid applause and preceded to do my thing – entertain with a good story.

Not only can I write a good story, I hear good stories. Have you heard the one about the three little old ladies who refused to admit they were hard of hearing? They were standing at the bus stop. The first lady said, "Boy, its windy today."

To which the second replied, "It's not Wednesday, it's Thursday."

"I'm thirsty too," said the third women, "Let's go have a cup of tea!" Needless to say they missed the bus.

OK, so it wasn't three little old ladies, it was three "old" friends and me!

My son recently bought a house. He said he was anxious to fill it. One day he called me and said, "Mother, I have great news. We are adding to our family." He and his lovely wife have been married for two years.

I was elated. This was indeed good news.

"I'm so excited," I said.

"We are too," he said. "His name is Louie."

"Louie?" I questioned.

"A Morris cat," he said. "You're going to love him, Mom."

I do love Louie. He's not quite what I was expecting my son to be expecting, but he is a lovable cat.

A few months later (or maybe it was a few weeks) the phone rang again.

"Mother," my son began…

"Let me guess. Another grandcat?"

"Yes, " I could almost hear him smiling. "His name is Jinx and you're going to love him. He's so adorable."

And Jinx is adorable. He kind of grows on you. I babysat him (or would that be cat sat?) for a few days while his owners were out of town. Jinx was a preemie. The mother cat died shortly after giving birth leaving Jinx and his fellow kittens' orphans. He was hand fed and grew up thinking he was a "real" baby and believe me, this cat knows he's adorable!

I still remember the first time I saw Jinx; he fit in the palm of my hand. We were having a rummage sale; my daughter-in-law couldn't leave him home alone so she brought him along to the sale. We laughed ourselves silly watching him trying to climb and/or jump from one arm of the chair to the other – it was hilarious. He was quite a hit with patrons coming and going. When he was delivered to our home for the weekend he came with a schedule which caused a few chuckles to remain on pursed lips.

"A schedule," my husband said. "His feeding times…" he

pointed to the list, along with two packages of dry food that had to be crushed, ground and mixed with water. Did I mention heating it in the microwave? Because he was so small he had to be fed several times a day (thus the schedule of feeding times) and watered since he preferred to bathe in his water bowl rather than drink from it! He came with his own penthouse kennel, feeding dish, water bowl, blanket and cat toys. Amazing.

"He goes to bed at ten," my husband said.

"Right." I nodded.

"And don't forget to bond with him," my son reminded us upon leaving.

"Right." I nodded again.

"To bed at ten…bond…crush and ground the food. Got it."

Jinx required a lot of attention and he got that from my husband who "bonded" with him in the evening. They watched TV together. Well, Bill watched TV. Jinx used that time to explore. And it was Bill who took the feeding times and cleaned the litter box. My main job was to play with Jinx and to teach him that he really wasn't a baby but a cat. I would open his cage and let him out to play in the kitchen, which we had blocked off from the rest of the house. We amused ourselves watching Jinx trying to jump over the huge cardboard barriers. It didn't take too long before we had to put up bigger barriers. And he got used to cuddling rather quickly and would whine and cry when we put him down for the night. (Long after ten and sometimes way before ten) It got to the point where I had to cover his cage so he'd think we'd gone to bed.

When my son came to collect his charge he was amazed at the string of toys, (empty pill bottles were his favorite) and cereal boxes, all over the floor. And by this time Jinx could climb in and out of his cage quite well. He had pretty much mastered being a cat.

"This!" my son said, "is going to be a problem, Mom. We don't let Jinx out of his cage."

"You do now," I laughed. That was the end (except for night-time) of Jinx being confined to his penthouse. He had learned to climb and whine. And he had learned to chew and to bite. Yes, we spoiled him rotten and sent him home. I think we'll make great grandparents!

Then along came Wendell, the dog. Part terrier, part bull. A rather strange-looking, but lovable dog. Wendell is nothing more than a big baby. Sometimes, I think he thinks he's one of the cats! Since I really do hate dogs, I had resolved not to like Wendell, but the problem is Wendell likes people and he especially likes me. Still, on my first few bonding with the dog visits, I would want Wendell in his cage. Not that I was afraid of him being a dog, but more so of him being an overly excitable dog. I didn't want him to knock me off my feet and have someone pick me up. So, in the cage he would go. The problem is he looked so darn pitiful in that cage. I mean, he's my granddog. You don't cage your granddog, do you? Somehow I knew that I would have to come to terms with Wendell and eventually I did.

One day when I was holding Louie and playing with Jinx, Wendell jumped up into my lap swatted the cats out of his way as if to say, "Wendell is here."

"Matt!" I yelled. "Get this dog off me, now!"

I loved Wendell, but a lap dog he is not.

Then, one summer day, there was Bailey; a lovable but dumb Beagle. Matt went out for dog food and came home with a dog to eat it!

Now that I've learned the art of bonding with my son's pets, I am hoping that before too long I will get a phone call and he will be adding a human to his family. I can only hope. In the meantime, I will wait for a call from my daughter to tell me she's engaged! Or that I have a grandfish!

One good thing about having a pet. They do help with the art of telling a good story.

The Truth about Cats and Dogs

And the myths.

Don't tell anyone, (not that I would ever want another pet) but there are moments in my life when I miss our cat King Tut. He's been gone a long time now. I'm still writing and telling stories about that darn cat.

I like to think God has a special place in heaven for the animals that He created. After all, they were created before man and I don't believe God would throw any part of his creation to the dogs (pardon the pun). If He does have a place in heaven for pets, I'm sure I'll see our cat Tut again…I hope so. We need animals in our lives…I know I do. Where would I get my animal stories if I couldn't write about people and their pets?

Have you ever wondered what a dog thinks? I bet if they could write and keep a personal journal it would read something like this:

    8:00 am - *Dog food! My favorite thing!*
    9:30 am - *A car ride! My favorite thing!*
    9:40 am - *A walk in the park! My favorite thing!*
    10:30 am - *Got rubbed and petted! My favorite thing!*
    12:00 pm - *Lunch! My favorite thing!*
    1:00 pm - *Played in the yard! My favorite thing!*
    3:00 pm - *Wagged my tail! My favorite thing!*
    5:00 pm - *Milk bones! My favorite thing!*
    7:00 pm - *Got to play ball! My favorite thing!*
    8:00 pm - *Watched TV with the people! My favorite thing!*
    11:00 pm - *Sleeping on the bed! My favorite thing!*

Excerpts from a Cat's Daily Diary:

Day 683 of my captivity: My captors continue to taunt me with bizarre little dangling objects. They dine lavishly on fresh meat, while the other inmates and I are fed hash or some sort of dry nuggets. Although I make my contempt for the rations perfectly clear, I nevertheless must eat something in order to keep up my strength. The only thing that keeps me going is my dream of escape.

In an attempt to disgust them, I once again vomit on the floor. Today I decapitated a mouse and dropped its headless body at their feet. I had hoped this would strike fear into their hearts, since it clearly demonstrates of what I am capable of. However, they merely made condescending comments about what a "good little hunter" I am. The audacity! There was some sort of assembly of their accomplices tonight. I was placed in solitary confinement for the duration of the event. However, I could hear the noises and smell the food. I overheard that my confinement was due to the power of "allergies." I must learn what this means, and how to use it to my advantage.

Today I was almost successful in an attempt to assassinate one of my tormentors by weaving around his feet as he was walking. I must try this again tomorrow but at the top of the stairs. The dog receives special privileges. He is regularly released - and seems to be more than willing to return. He is obviously retarded! The bird has got to be an informant. I observe him communicating with the guards regularly. I am certain that he reports my every move. My captors have arranged protective custody for him in an elevated cell, so he is safe... for now. Tomorrow is another day...I will write again soon.

The difference between cats and dogs is quite obvious. Dogs only think they are people – cats know it! Like I said, pets are always good for a story. Thank you God for making them! (I think).

(Thank you to my Internet friends for help in writing this article.)

God Works in Mysterious Ways

Thank goodness He doesn't let us in on the mysteries of life.

Thanks to sensationalism by the media we hear a lot more about life's traumas and dramas then necessary. Drive-by shootings and terrorism in the schools seem to be the norm these days. It's getting to the point where you can't trust anyone not even your own brother! It's good to read about the positives; at least we know when good things happen that God is still in control. He can take a bad situation and turn it into something good—our knee bending has not been in vain.

You never know when you pray what God will do. The following story is a perfect example of the mysterious but wondrous ways of God.

A woman received a phone call from her sitter that her daughter was sick with a high fever.

She left work and stopped by the pharmacy for medication. Returning to her car, she found she had locked her keys inside. She didn't know what to do. She called her home to talk to the sitter, and was told her daughter was getting worse.

The sitter said, "Look around and see if you can find something to open the door. The woman found an old rusty coat hanger on the ground, then looked at the hanger and said, "I don't know how to use this." Not knowing what else to do, she bowed her head and asked God for help.

An old car pulled up, driven by a dirty, greasy, bearded man with a biker skull rag on his head. The woman thought, "Great God. This is who you sent to help me?" But she was desperate, and thankful. The man got out of his car and asked if he could help.

"Yes, my daughter is very sick. I must get home to her. Please, can you use this hanger to unlock my car? "

"Sure," said the man. "No problem." He walked over to the car and in seconds the car door was opened.

She hugged the man and through her tears said, "Thank you so much. You are a very nice man."

"Lady," he said, "I am not a nice man. I just got out of prison for car theft."

The woman hugged him again and cried out loud, "THANK YOU, GOD FOR SENDING ME A PROFESSIONAL!"

Sometimes God sends help in the most unusual ways. When I was in my 20s, I did something really stupid. I picked up a hitchhiker and much to my dismay he highjacked my cousin, my just-paid-for car and me!

"Help me, Lord!" I cried out. Help came in the form of my mother's homemade chicken soup. The fact that I'm a storyteller and couldn't keep my mouth shut probably saved our lives. I rattled on about my Mom's chicken soup, how she had just made it that morning, the ingredients, etc. The soup was in a container in the backseat of the car. I didn't want it to spoiled and thought we should pull over and eat the soup! In spite of the fact that our kidnapper and car thief had a gun, I kept talking to him about one thing or another to the point of where he became confused. At one point he dropped the gun. I don't know how I did it, but I managed to talk him into dropping us off on a deserted highway. Miraculously we escaped and lived to tell this story. As our assailant was driving away in my 65 Chevy Impala, I yelled, "Don't forget to eat the chicken soup!" Yes, I was still worried about Mom's soup.

The point is, (I can hear your thoughts) help always comes. Even in the mist of sensationalized drama and trauma, even in the mist of a foiled kidnapping attempt, where a good pot of chicken soup is spoiling, He will never leave us nor forsake us and there is nothing mysterious about that. God is good all the time.

A Rose in God's Garden

A rose by any other name is still a rose.

A young priest was walking in the garden one day, with an older, more seasoned priest. The inexperienced priest was feeling a bit insecure about what God had for him to do. He decided to ask the older priest for some advice. The older gentlemen walked up to a rose bush and handed the young priest a rosebud and told him to open it without tearing any of the petals. The young priest looked in disbelief at the older priest, trying to figure out what a rosebud could possibly have to do with his wanting to know the will of God for his life and ministry. But, because of his great respect for the older priest, he proceeded to try and unfold the rosebud while keeping every petal intact. It wasn't long before he realized how impossible this was to do. Noticing the young priest's inability to unfold the rosebud without tearing it, the older priest began to recite the following poem:

> It is only a tiny rosebud
> A flower of God's design;
> But I cannot unfold the petals
> With these clumsy hands of mine.
> The secret of unfolding flowers
> Is not known to such as I.
> GOD opens this flower so sweetly,
> Then, in my hands, they die.
> If I cannot unfold a rosebud,
> The flower of God's design,

> Then how can I have the wisdom
> To unfold this life of mine?
> So, I'll trust in Him for leading
> Each moment of my day.
> I will look to Him for His guidance
> Each step of the Pilgrim's way
> The pathway that lies before me
> Only my Heavenly Father knows.
> I'll trust him to unfold the moments,
> Just as He unfolds the rose.

How many times have you said to yourself, "If there are so many roses in the garden of life, how come I get all the thorns?" If anyone is going to find a picker among the flowers it's me! But I don't mind because I can make a story out of anything – even a weed!

Sometimes, our path in life seems difficult to follow at best, but we can trust in our Heavenly Father to know what's best for us. For He knows what lies ahead and like a rose, He will reveal and unfold those special moments in our lives. All we need to do is trust in Him and live each day in faith knowing that we are a rose in God's garden. And if you come to the garden alone while the dew is still on the roses, He will walk with you and talk with you and you will know what to do with your life. One thing I know for sure, you'll stop seeing the thorns and allow the beauty of the rose to appear. Even among the weeds a flower grows—get down, get dirty and pull those weeds!

Trusting Jesus

Day by day trust and obey.

Growing up isn't easy for anyone; it especially wasn't easy for me. I was born with cerebral palsy. Growing up in the 40s there was no such thing as "physically challenged" you were the crippled kid and you had to learn to deal with it.

When other kids made fun of me, my mother would say, "Trust Jesus."

Determined that I would learn how to ride a bike, when I would fall off Mom would say, "Get back on and try again."

"I'm afraid," I'd whine.

"Trust Jesus," she would say.

It didn't matter what trial I was going through, the advice was always the same. I grew up a tough kid – trusting Jesus.

With all that's going on in the world these days trusting Jesus is not always easy to do. Trials and tribulations bring to mind an old hymn written by Edgar Stites. A song our Bible study group sang at one of our meetings not so long ago. This song made me realize the value of trusting in our Lord and Savior to calm the storms of life. And believe me, I have gone through many a storm. I haven't walked on water, but I know that I can if I simply trust.

"Simply trusting every day; Trusting through a stormy way; Even when my faith is small, trusting Jesus that is all.

Trusting as the moments fly; Trusting as the days go by; Trusting Him what-e'er befall, trusting Jesus that is all."

Stites, a direct descendent of John Howland, one of the

passengers of the Mayflower, was born in 1836 and died in 1921. In his 85 years of life, he served in the Civil War and was a river boat pilot before becoming a missionary on the frontier in North Dakota. Stites wrote *Trusting Jesus* as a poem, which appeared in a local newspaper of his time. Evangelist, D.L. Moody happened to see the poem and ask his soloist and song leader, Ira Sankey, to put music to the words. It was copyrighted in 1904.

Trusting Jesus," a hymn that is completely American in background, expresses the motive and purpose of life; living a practical Christian life by trusting God's mercy and grace for each day. Through every trial we ever face, we must remember Ephesians 2:8, "For by grace you are saved through faith." As great as that verse is, Hebrews 10:38 speaks to my heart, "Now the just shall live by faith." This, my friends," said Billy Graham in his telling of this hymn story, " is the secret of living the Christian life -- every day faith -- trusting Him in everything we do."

"Brightly doth His Spirit shine
Into this poor heart of mine;
While He leads I cannot fail;
Trusting Jesus, that is all.
Singing if my way is clear;
Praying if the path is drear;
If in danger, for Him call;
Trusting Jesus, that is all.
Trusting Him while life shall last;
Trusting Him till earth be past;
Till within the jasper wall;
Trusting Jesus that is all..."

God is in control. All He asks of us is that we trust Him.

The Still Small Voice of God

Hello, are you there?

Sometimes we humans get so busy we forget what the still small voice of God actually sounds like. We want God to speak to us, but in the comings and goings of everyday living we forget to stop and listen. I am not the only one guilty of this.

I have had friends ask "God, speak to me." All the while they are surrounded with the beautiful sounds of the meadowlarks on a balmy spring day, and the croaking of frogs on a warm summer night. I remember such sounds in lazy hazy days of summer during my youth. As I grew into adulthood, the sounds were less noticeable. The problem is, in our business we don't always hear. We often fail to notice the little things.

Sometimes I get so frustrated I can hear myself yell, "God, speak to me!" How can I be expected to hear God above the roar of rolling thunder? Or the crackling of lightening? Or the lauger of giggling children?

Have you ever seen God? Would you recognize Him if you saw Him? "God let me see you," should be our cry every day. To see God, to know Him, to reach out and touch Him.

I have seen God. We all have. He's there in the light of a star, in the crescent of a moon, in the beauty of a new born baby. He's in the smile of a child's face and in the early morning dew that graces the morning glories. His voice is there if we just come to the garden.

"I don't think I've ever seen a miracle," my husband commented one day.

"Yes, you have," I reminded him. "Life is a miracle."

"You know what I mean," he said. "I'm talking about a touch from God." He gently brushed a butterfly away and walked on.

"Touch me God, and let me know you are here." I smiled as I watched the bees, the birds, the butterflies and playing children. All a sign of the miracle of life. All alive because of God's touch.

God is always around us in the little and simple things that we take for granted even in our electronic age, so I would like to add one more: "God, I need your help!"

Just about the time I think God's not listening, I get a phone call or an e-mail from a friend reaching out with good news and words of encouragement. Next time you get such an e-mail, don't delete it and continue crying, "God where are you?"

He's been here all the time waiting for you to recognize that still small voice. Take time to listen. Don't miss out on a blessing because it isn't packaged the way that you expected to be.

Good Old Fashion Hymn Sing

I love to sing the story.

I included this story in my book just for the fun of it. Sometimes, something really good comes across the Internet and finds its way into my e-mail box. This was one of those times for me. When this message came to me it was too good not to share.

Every church needs to host a good old fashion hymn sing every now and then. If you or your church is thinking of hosting such an event, let me help you in your hymn selection. Be sure to include a hymn for everyone. Your program could be comprised of the following hymns:

> The Dentist's Hymn – Crown Him with Many Crowns
> The Weatherman's Hymn – There Shall Be Showers
>   of Blessings
> The Contractor's Hymn – The Church's One Foundation
> The Tailor's Hymn – Holy, Holy, Holy
> The Golfer's Hymn – There Is a Green Hill Far Away
> The Politician's Hymn – Standing on the Promises
> The Optometrist's Hymn – Open My Eyes That I Might See
> The IRS Agent's Hymn – I Surrender All
> The Gossip's Hymn – Pass It On
> The Electrician's Hymn – Send the Light
> The Shopper's Hymn – Sweet By and By
> The Realtor's Hymn – I Got a Mansion Just over the Hilltop

And for the motorists:
- 55 mph – Guide Me, O Thou Great Jehovah
- 65 mph – Nearer My God to Thee
- 75 mph – Nearer Still Nearer
- 85 mph – This World Is Not My Home
- 95 mph – Lord, I'm Coming Home
- Over 100 mph – Precious Memories

Next time your church is hosting an old fashion hymn sing and if you think about inviting me. I love to sing! And besides, my mother said, "singing is good for you!"

(This article first appeared in The Crossroads Newspaper, 2003.)

What I Still Don't Know About Diet & Exercise

I know I'm not good at it!

I've been on a diet since the day I was born! This is true. I've lost the same 30 pounds four times. That's 120 pounds. I should be looking good; instead I'm looking to see where I lost those pounds! Maybe it was K-Mart!

My doctor doesn't understand how anyone can spend $600 in two years trying to lose weight and still weigh the same as when the so-called diet began.

The answer is easy. It's the scales. Everyone who has ever been on a diet knows that scales vary. No two models weigh the same. And everybody's scale is different in looks, size and measurement. Is it my fault that someone out there cannot build good, durable and consistent scales? Universal scales if you will. And what about stress? It's so stressful to think of dieting that you're constantly eating! And the idea of a "life-style change" that scares me. Now, don't get me wrong. It may be true that I snack all day long but they are healthy WW snacks—Weight Watcher approved. I should know. I'm a lifetime weight watcher and I approve my snacks! My favorite: "light chips." What's not to love! Eat more for half the fat.

How did our society become so consumed with dieting? It certainly isn't part of God's plan because, in the beginning, when God created the heavens and the earth he populated the earth with broccoli, cauliflower, spinach, green and yellow and red vegetables of all kinds. He did this so man and woman would live long and healthy lives.

Then using God's great gifts, Satan created Ben and Jerry's Ice Cream and Krispy Creme Donuts. And Satan said, "You want chocolate with that?" And Man said, "Yes!" and Woman said, "as long as you're at it, add some sprinkles." And they gained 10 pounds. And Satan smiled. You know, I believe that obesity comes from the devil and I can picture him smiling every time someone gains a pound or five.

But God was ready. He created the healthful yogurt that woman might keep the figure that Man found so fair. And Satan brought forth white flour from the wheat, and sugar from the cane and combined them. And woman went from size 6 to size 14.

So God said, "Try my fresh green salad."

With or without Thousand Island dressing, buttery croutons and garlic toast on the side? Who said salads were a dieter's delight? Even a salad can cause mere man (and women) to unfasten their belts following the repast.

God does not give up. In his creation of a healthy eating plan, He said, "I have sent you heart healthy vegetables and olive oil in which to cook them." And Satan brought forth deep fried fish and chicken-fried steak so big it needed its own platter. And man gained more weight and his cholesterol went through the roof.

God then created a light, fluffy white cake, named it "Angel Food Cake," and said, "It is good." Satan then created chocolate cake and named it "Devil's Food."

OK – so you've eaten all this "stuff" things you know you shouldn't. There's still a chance to redeem yourself. God created running shoes so that His children might lose those extra pounds. And Satan gave cable TV with a remote control so man would not have to toil changing the channels. And man and woman laughed and cried before the flickering blue light while eating buttered microwave popcorn and gained pounds.

But then, God brought forth the potato naturally low in fat and brimming with nutrition. And Satan peeled off the healthful skin and sliced the starchy center into chips and deep-fried them. And man gained pounds. What! My chips are fattening? What's up with that?

God then gave lean beef so that man might consume fewer calories and still satisfy his appetite. And Satan created McDonald's and its 99-cent double cheeseburger. Then said, "You want fries with that?" And man replied, "Yes! And super sized them!" And Satan said, "It is good." And man went into cardiac arrest.

God sighed and created quadruple bypass surgery.

Then Satan created HMOs.

And man wonders when is all this madness going to end

Sooner than you might think!

The point of this story is: Early to bed. Early to rise. Man will live longer if he's healthy and wise! Satan is a deceiver – the king of all lies. Now off to bed with you and no snacking on the way!

"Work is love made visible."
—*Kahil Gibran*

Solving Problems Isn't Really That Difficult

All it takes is a good cup of coffee!

Everywhere I turn these days I see people concentrating on problems: illegal immigration, hurricane recovery, and wild animals attacking humans in Florida. What's the world coming to? As Christians shouldn't our focus be more on solutions to these problems?

It seems to me that the resolutions are staring us in the face and if applied we'd have a "win win" solution to at least three of the world's problems.

Illegal immigration wouldn't be a problem if we'd take the low-crime criminals (taking up jail space) and make them dig a moat the length of the Mexican border.

We can use the dirt to raise the levies in New Orleans. And then, we can put the Florida alligators in the moat! Problems solved.

When things in your life seem almost too much to handle, when 24 hours in a day are not enough, remember the mayonnaise jar and two cups of coffee. Let me explain:

A professor stood before his philosophy class and had some items in front of him. When the class began, he wordlessly picked up a very large and empty mayonnaise jar and proceeded to fill it with golf balls. He then asked the students if the jar was full. They agreed that it was.

The professor then picked up a box of pebbles and poured them into the jar. He shook the jar lightly. The pebbles rolled into the open areas between the golf balls. He then asked the students again if the jar was full. They agreed it was.

The professor next picked up a box of sand and poured it into the jar. Of course, the sand filled up everything else. He asked once more if the jar was full. The students responded with a unanimous "yes."

The professor then produced two cups of coffee from under the table and poured the entire contents into the jar effectively filling the empty space between the sand. The students laughed.

"Now," said the professor as the laughter subsided, "I want you to recognize that this jar represents your life. The golf balls are the important things--your family, your children, your health, your friends and your favorite passions---and if everything else was lost and only they remained, your life would still be full.

The pebbles are the other things that matter like your job, your house and your car. The sand is everything else---the small stuff. "If you put the sand into the jar first," he continued, "there is no room for the pebbles or the golf balls. The same goes for life. If you spend all your time and energy on the small stuff you will never have room for the things that are important to you.

"Pay attention to the things that are critical to your happiness. Play with your children. Take time to get medical checkups. Take your spouse out to dinner. Play another 18 holes of golf. There will always be time to clean the house and fix the disposal. Take care of the golf balls first---the things that really matter. Set your priorities. The rest is just sand."

One of the students raised her hand and inquired what the coffee represented. The professor smiled. "I'm glad you asked. It just goes to show you that no matter how full your life may seem, there's always room for a couple of cups of coffee with a friend."

Most of life's problems can be solved over a good cup of Java because problem solving begins with "listening." Any more problems I can solve?

(This article first appeared in His Banner Newspaper, 2007.)

What I Know About Men

What's to know?

My cousin gave me a little plague one year for my birthday that I absolutely love. It sits on a shelf in my office above my computer. "Sure God created Man before Woman…but then you always make a rough draft before the final MASTERPIECE."

I read all the books, including *"Men Are From Mars, Women are From Venus"* I still don't get it! Why did God make men and women so different?

Women are multi-taskers. We have to be. I don't know of any man who can cook, sew, talk on the phone, tend to little people and put clothes in the dryer all at the same time. Never send a man to the basement to get the laundry out of the clothes dryer and bring up the hamper at the same time. He'll forget why you sent him down there and come up with a can of beans! It's happened in our house.

And I don't get that men don't get romance. Women need it. Men don't get that. My mother used to say, "If you want romance, plan it yourself." So, one year I went all out on Valentine's Day. I planned a romantic dinner, bought myself a rose. Even called my husband at work to remind him, "It's Valentine's Day."

I told him to meet me at our favorite restaurant. Actually I instructed that he come home from work an hour early, shower, shave, change his clothes and then meet me at the restaurant at 4:30 PM on the dot. I got there at 4 PM. I was all decked out… wearing red, got the heart earrings going on. I'm smelling like a rose and stewing like an onion in a crock-pot! It was 5 PM, no date. He's late. I hate tardiness.

He finally shows up, but not dressed up. He just doesn't get it. He slides into the romantic back booth I told the waitress I needed looking like he just got out of work and I'm sure he worked overtime. Blue jeans, flannel shirt, shop glasses still on his nose—you know the kind--the ones with those little blinders on the side. Yeah, I really hate those. There's nothing remotely romantic about those glasses.

"So what's up?" he wants to know.

"It's Valentine's Day," I remind him "I'm in the mood."

"For a steak?"

Right.

"You're looking spiffy." Our waitress smiles at me as she sits two glasses of water in front of us.

"What's up with him?" Hubby gets an imposing eye. I bet she's wondering why I asked for the back booth. Romance, I remind myself.

It gets worse. Now we are at home. (I told the boy to stay away until at least 9 PM). "What are these?" he asks.

"What do they look like?"

"Boxer shorts, with hearts, ooooh. I don't wear these."

"I know." I wink or at least I make an attempt at winking. (I cannot wink, I can twitch. That's about it.)

"Something wrong with your eye?" he asks.

"I'm thinking romance." I smile. "I have the other half of that outfit. Shall I go and slip…"

"No," he says.

"No?" I'm perplexed. "No."

"I have to go into work at 2am tomorrow. I need to get some sleep."

Just then the phone rings. It's the boy. He's having car trouble and wants to talk to his dad. They chitchat for several long minutes.

"You have to go pick Matt up in Midland," my husband tells me. "I have to go to bed."

"What about Valentine's Day? What about love and romance?"

"Can we celebrate it later? I have to go to bed."

Going to bed…isn't that what I had planned all along? Or not.

Men! I just don't get that they don't get it.

I guess it doesn't matter. Men are happy the way they are. What do you expect from such simple creatures?

I mean think about it. Their last name stays put. You don't see a man changing his last name to the woman's now do you? Some of us opt to keep our maiden names, but few men, none that I know, change their names to ours. And it's never "Mrs. And Mr." It's always, "Mr. and Mrs." The garage is all theirs. Heaven help you if you "dare" to go out there and clean it. Do not. I repeat, do not invade their territory.

Wedding plans take care of themselves. At least as far as most grooms-to-be are concerned, ours did. I have yet to see a man get excited over color choices and whether or not you should have the white sheet going down the isle. Do they really care? Why is it that we women have to pay big bucks for a wedding dress while men pay $100 to rent a tux! What's fair about that?

And to my husband, chocolate is just another snack. He doesn't understand a women's craving for the hard stuff—I'm talking dark chocolate ladies. Men can be President. They never have to worry about getting pregnant, stretch marks or their boobs eventually sagging to their knees.

They can wear a white T-shirt to a water park—or NO shirt to a water park.

Car mechanics tell the truth when they see you're with a man; what's that all about? I have a girlfriend who's actually a better mechanic than her husband! Ever notice, the world is a man's urinal. They never have to drive to another gas station because the restroom in the last one was just too "icky." And, men don't have to stop and think of which way to turn a nut on a bolt. They do the same job as a woman for more pay. Wrinkles add character. People never stare at their chest when talking to a man. The occasional well-rendered belch is not only appreciated by males and their counterparts, but practically expected.

New shoes don't cut, blister, or mangle their feet. One thing I notice about men is that they have "one" mood all the time. Phone conversations are over in 30 seconds flat and they know stuff about tanks and guns how to trap a varmint. But ask them their opinion about something serious and they haven't a clue.

A five-day vacation requires only one suitcase per man. Is it like they forget to pack their underwear? You almost never see a strap wrinkle in men's clothing once it's out of the suitcase. Why is that? Men can open all their own jars and they get extra credit for the slightest act of thoughtfulness. If someone forgets to invite a man to a party, he or she can still be your friend. It takes woman months to get over not being invited to a party.

You know something else I don't get? A man can put a shirt on with or without a tie and look great. Underwear is $8.95 for a three-pack. Three pairs of shoes are more than enough for any man and you hardly ever hear them complain that their feet hurt. Hey, Bub – why don't you try walking round in 4" heels! Everything on a man's face stays its original color. The same hairstyle lasts for years, maybe decades. They only have to shave their face and neck and then they have the nerve to wonder why it takes us women so long to get ready to go anywhere. Men can play with toys all of their lives. (They graduate from boy toys to "man" toys.). Truthfully, they never really grow up. Their belly usually hides big hips. One wallet, one pair of shoes one color for all seasons. It seems unfair to me that men can wear shorts no matter how their legs look. They can "do" their nails with a pocket knife. They have freedom of choice concerning growing a mustache. Some of us have facial hair we neither want nor need.

And what really grinds me is the fact that a man can do Christmas shopping for twenty five relatives on December 24 in 25 minutes. No wonder men are happier than we are! Life's a bowl of cherries.

(Thanks to help from my Internet friends in writing this article.)

THINK
of Becoming a Giver of Joy

I find that I have a lot more amazing days if I don't think too much. When I think about how much time I waste "thinking" it boggles my mind. I think about what I should have done…could have done…should be doing. I think about the outcome of my thoughts…if I would have done things different…if I had rationalized and reasoned. The big thing on my mind at the moment is joy. How do I become a joy giver?

What is joy? How do you get it? And how do you give it away? Joy: Pleasure. Extreme gladness. A thing (or person) who causes joy. To be joyful: "full of showing joy or causing joy." (Oxford American Dictionary).

Romans 12:8 talks about the gift of exhortation. As Christians we are supposed to be exhorters, encouraging one another, building one another up. (I Thessalonians 5:11). I think when we become exhorters, joy happens. It's how we show joy. When a child has been hurt, criticized, picked on – the words you say or don't say and how you say them can have a lasting effect on that child's life. You can be the cause of joyfulness or sorrow.

My mother could be verbally abusive at times. I don't think she realized the impact or the sting that the words she'd often hurl at us growing up, had on our emotional growth – our self-worth. An encouraging word spoken at just the right moment can bring joy and raise you up to new levels; a hurtful word spoken anytime can bring you down, making you feel worthless and unworthy of love. We all need to guard our tongues and be careful how we speak to one another. We don't want to become robbers of joy.

Not only do the words you say have a lasting affect but the decisions you make affect everyone around you. The words you speak, the way you say them, the decisions you make not only affect your family and friends it can affect your attitude toward spiritual matters and in the end affect your relationship with God. Not having a good relationship with God can rob you of joy.

I find myself thinking too much about things that really don't matter when I really need to focus on the effect of what I am doing (or not doing) will have on others. In one of Joyce Meyer's books she said: "*Learn to think for yourself. Don't let other people do your thinking.*" I am very good at letting other people think for me. This way I have someone else to blame when I mess up! And by letting others think for me, tell me how to feel, act, dress – I don't have to take responsibility for the negative energy I allow into my life. I've looked at life from both sides, from win and lose....I guess it's like that old John Davison song says, "*...It's false illusions I recall, I really don't know life at all.*"

I want to be a joy giver – not a joy sapper. Negative words cause a multitude of "don't wants" in my life. As a Christian I don't want (nor do I need) my life to be crowded with non-spiritual lifestyles. I want to be Christ-like. A giver of comfort and joy – someone that people want to be around because I make them feel good.

Those that write self-help books will be the first to tell you that the mind is a powerful thing; if only we as Christians would realize the power we have, could have, if we just tap into His power source. We need to learn how to pray believing we'll receive something good from God.

Having recently sold my publishing business, I had a choice to make. I could wallow in what was (which I did for months) or forget the past and start over with a heart of gratitude, joy and thanksgiving; thanking God for everything He taught me about running a business, realizing those were good times, but now I need to take affirmative action and move on with my life to create more good times.

We all want peace, happiness and joy in our lives, right? Don't you want to be happy in everything you do? I do. My biggest problem is I'm never quite sure what makes me happy. I need to go back to that chapter on "What is Happiness" and read it again!

When I teach a Creative Writing class, I always ask my students to make a list of why they want to write and another list on what makes them happy. Nine times out of ten, writing is on the happy list. Writing makes me more than happy – it fills my heart with joy. It's through my writing that I know I can give some of my joy away!

"Happiness I have discovered is nearly always a rebound of hard work."
—*David Grayson*

Looking for Peace in All the Wrong Places

His peace passes all understanding.

The most profound thing you can ever do for yourself is to find peace, His peace, the peace that passes all understanding.

"How do I find peace?" I had a friend ask once. "My life is in so much turmoil I don't think I would recognize peace if it bite me in the butt."

I have the same problem. For me, peace began with forgiveness. If you are harboring unforgiveness against yourself or somebody else, start by forgiving yourself first and then forgiving others. It comes through making a conscious effort to make changes in whatever phase of your life is causing you stress. Stress, resentment, bitterness, worry are not friends of peace.

For me finding the path of my peace didn't come from forgiveness alone. I had to discipline myself to make some changes in my life. I had to let go of stress, but first I had to figure out what and who was causing the stress. I came to the realization rather quickly that I am my own worst enemy.

As hard as this concept may be to grasp, especially if you are not at peace – is change what's bad in your life to good. Liberate yourself by making the wrongs in your life – the rights. There is a right way to think and act and do. It may begin with developing a positive attitude. Positivity breeds peace.

The most important thing you can do in your quest for peace is to learn what is true. Know the truth and you will be free, that's what the Word of God says. (John 8:32)

What are the truths in your life that keep you from peace? Allow God to be in control of your life path. Let Him be the director in your life. Life is not meant to be a struggle; it's meant to be joyfully abundant. You will never have peace until you have peace with yourself and peace with God. God is in us. We are in God – if we have that concept down – the rest will be easy.

I Don't Know Much about Aging—Yet

The art of growing old gracefully.

I don't worry as much about birthdays as I used to. There going to come whether I want them to or not. I suppose having a birthday is better than the alternative. The one thing I have learned about celebrating those "over 50" birthdays is that "aging" seems to come along with having a birthday. We can't do anything about that, either.

I cannot believe what I see when I look in the mirror – my mother! You heard me right. I have turned into my mother. I laugh like her, walk like her. I'm saying and doing all the things she used to do. I am my mother reincarnated.

It wasn't that long ago that my cousin and I laughed at our mothers, sitting around the dining table like a bunch of "old" hens. (Not that "hens" sit around a dining table.) I think they called themselves the "Ladies Aid Society" or the "Ladies Extension" or something like that. They were knitting of all things. I will never knit, ever! Nope, it's not who I am.

We were pre-teens talking about rock stars and make-up; they were seniors talking about rock gardens and making up a Sunday menu, who had the most aches and labor pains. We were horrified that upstanding women of the church would talk so vulgar, thinking what a pain they were!

"Hopefully, we're never going to be there, doing that. We are NOT going to talk about our surgeries or our babies." We promised one another.

Now, we promise one another that we'll go to the home together! And we have both had our gall bladders out! And yes, we talk about it!

My cousin said her car was getting old and that she was thinking about trading it in. I feel like a car sometimes. Wish I could trade my body in for a new one.

"What's wrong with your car? I had to ask.

"Bumps," she said, "where there shouldn't be any—and dents and scratches. The windows won't open. The horn doesn't work. The body is worn out."

"I have the same problem with my body," I laughed, only it wasn't funny.

We trade our cars in but we're pretty much stuck with our old bodies, bumps, dents and all. But that's not the worst of it. My eyes are out of focus. What's up with that? It's especially hard to see close up. Come to think of it, I don't see so good far away, either. I can't drive at night anymore, everything's fuzzy.

"I don't know what's wrong with my car. The traction's not so good, anymore and it takes hours to reach maximum speed," my cousin was explaining.

"Same here," I mumbled.

"What's that?" she said. "Hearing's going?"

"Tell me about it. I don't hear. I don't see. My traction isn't as graceful as it once was. I slip and slide, skid and bump into things."

"Me too," she said.

This I know; I used to depend on my cousin to help me get around. She's been my aid all my life and now we have to help each other cross the street. She and I are in the same boat and it's sinking. Our bodies need an overhaul; our legs are stained with varicose veins and talk about reaching maximum speed. It takes forever just to walk from the kitchen to the bathroom!

"I don't get good gas mileage anymore," she sighed.

"Who does?"

"What?"

"What you mean what?"

There was a long pause of silence.

"I can't hear you…"

"I stopped talking." I mouthed.

You know the worst thing about getting old? Almost every time I sneeze, cough or sputter, either my radiator leaks or my exhausts backfires! Yep, it's definitely time for a trade in!

Living Life as a Grown-up

Isn't all that much fun.

It's funny when you're a kid, you can't wait to be a grownup. When you're a kid, it takes forever to live life. When you're three, you want to be six and go to school. When you finally get in school, you want that part of your life over so you can get a car, a job a life of your own.

When you finally become a grownup, you wish you were a kid again. It's a lot more fun being a kid! Life as a grownup is short lived.

When you're a kid, you're on the go all the time; it doesn't seem like a kid allows much time for enjoying anything but coming and going. They're too busy.

Life is too short to be so busy. One should learn the art of becoming unbusy. The only way to do that is to take more breaks. Walk a garden path, smell the roses, enjoy a good cup of coffee out on the back porch. Sit and watch your neighbors. Better yet, actually visit your neighbor. Don't let weeds choke the path to your neighbor's house.

When you're a kid growing up there seems to be too many rules. You have to get up at a certain time, go to bed at a certain time, eat and clean your room, and practice your piano lessons. Kids today are on a tighter schedule than their parents are. It's amazing they have time to walk the dog. Oh, that's right, I walk the dog!

I've come to the conclusion living life as a grownup that it's OK to break the rules once in awhile. Let your kids break the rules once in awhile, too – it could be fun. So who cares if the room isn't cleaned exactly to your perfections? And who said you can't go on a picnic in the middle of the week on a rainy day? And splashing through the mud can be fun.

The best thing you can do living life as a grownup is to be a kid again; forgive quickly. Forget harboring grudges and nursing old wounds. Life is far too short to worry about the past. Get over it.

Kiss slowly. Savor the tenderness of a kiss, the passion of knowing someone still loves you enough to want to kiss you. Love truly and deeply and never forget the importance of saying those three little words, "I love you." Say those words to your children and say them often. Every day say "I love you" to your spouse, your parents, your siblings, your friends. Faith, hope and love; love is the greatest of these.

Laugh uncontrollably. Laughter is good medicine and it's contagious. And never ever regret anything that made you smile.

You know if you practice these things every day, living life as a grown-up isn't all that bad.

Sing Out

A good parenting tip.

When I was a kid and would get in a grumpy mood, my mother would tell me to "sing out;" – sing out the grumpies, sing out the blues, depression, the anxieties of life – whatever was going on she believed you could solve it with a song.

It's a principle I applied when raising my own children. If they had a problem, I'd tell them to sing out. I have found you cannot be sad and sing a happy song at the same time. It just doesn't work. Maybe that's why God places so much credence on "praise."

Got a problem? Turn on the music. Turn up the music. Sing, dance, and flood your soul with joy. Praise His Holy name by giving Him praise through the music He has created. Be joyful in your everyday life. If you're depressed, be delighted; if you're sad, shout away your sadness; if you're angry, be angelic; if you anxious, be anticipating; if you're lonely go out and share your joy with others!

You cannot be sad, lonely, depressed or anxious when you sing out!

More good tips:

If your children like to argue, make them sit in chairs facing one another and give each other compliments for 35 minutes. They will soon abandoned negative terms of endearment as they learn to replace them with positive words of encouragement!

My husband said that he and his brothers never said, "I'm bored" when Mother was around, "because," he said, "she put us to work twiddling our thumbs." Now, that's boring. His dad would go one better and give him a hoe and tell him to go hoe beans!

Maybe that's what's wrong with kids today – too much time wasted sitting in front of the computer and not enough time spent outdoors hoeing beans! Or pulling weeds, or watering the garden, mowing the grass – whatever it takes, get those kids out of the house. If they insist on doing otherwise, instruct them in the art of thumb twiddling!

There is No Fear...

In the perfect love of God.

Now that I am officially retired from business, I'm wondering what the next step is? I know that I'm not finished yet, that God still has "things" for me to do. I just have to figure out what those things are. And what's holding me back.

I said to a friend recently, "I should get a part time job."

"You're kidding me, right?" my friend responded incredulously.

"Well, not really."

"You have a part time job," she reminded me. "You're a writer – that's your job."

She's right, of course.

My God given gift is to write. When I was in publishing, my efforts were concentrated on helping other authors publish their books; my own dream to write gone by the wayside. I was never meant to be the president of a publishing company. That was my business partner's dream. One that he gave up much too soon, as far as I'm concerned. But I did learn a valuable lesson; you can't go through life living someone else's dream. You won't be happy. My dream is to write. And although I tell the world I am retired, I don't think we ever retire from God's service, doing what it is that He wants us to do. I have a destiny to fulfill – to write another book and another. So what's holding me back? Fear.

"Sometimes," my friend told me, "we need to step outside of our comfort zone in order to accomplish all that God has planned for us."

Perhaps, what I need to do in order to accomplish the goals set before me is to examine my heart and soul, to discover if fear is my enemy! Then, hand my fears and discouragements over to the One who loves me more than anyone else! God. There is no fear in the perfect love of God.

I just need to remind myself of that fact from time to time as I tell myself, "I can do this." Soak up all the strength and courage He has to give and move forward! In Christ all things are possible. Even another book!

Does God Take Vacations?

I hope not.

"Mom, does God take vacations?" my daughter asked one day. She was three at the time.

"I don't think so," I said. "Why do you ask?"

"Because," she said, "I pray and pray and God forgets to answer me so I figure He's on vacation."

That simple statement made me chuckle.

I wonder how many others out there, both child and adult, feel sometimes as if God is on vacation. I can assure you He is not. God is alive and working in our lives, 24/7, to make sure that our needs are being met.

Maybe I'm the problem. Am I talking to God on a regular basis? Do I thank Him every day for the things He has provided for me? Do I praise or complain? Am I letting God know what I need? And do I only go to him when I have a need?

I think of God in the same way I think of a friend. No one wants to hang around with me if all I ever do is ask something from them, complain about my problems all the time, grumble about my health. I go to physical therapy from time to time. It's a real wake up call. I see people with real needs. Instead of thinking about myself and what I need I used that bike pedaling time to intercede for others. I'm really in good shape for the shape that I'm in! In those moments, I realize that God is not on vacation and that I have everything I need.

What is your relationship with God like? God has given us every opportunity to know Him on a personal basis. How Wonderful! I don't know about you, but I'm placing my trust in Him who loves me with an unending love. Makes it easier to follow Him, don't you agree?

Next time you're on vacation, don't forget to take God with you!

Givers and Takers

Which one are you?

My mother was a giver. She'd give you the jacket off her back if she thought you needed it. If you went into her home and you commented, "This is nice, where did you get it?" It was yours. She was generous to a fault.

Mom always told me, "Give and you will get back twice what you gave." I'm not sure at the time she realized this was a biblical principle. "A good measure, pressed down, shaken together and running over, will be poured into your lap; give and it will be given to you." I've heard many versions of this principle.

I had a great uncle, a wealthy man, who had a lot of money. A lot of it he gave away, but he horded a lot of it, too. When he got sick, his family asked him what he would do with his money.

"Just worry about it, I guess," he told them.

My husband is a lot like that uncle. He seems to worry about his "stuff". He has so much "stuff" that in order to get the basement and garage cleaned, we had to actually build a new house and with it came a pole barn to keep all his "stuff" in. It reminds me of that kid book *The Stuff Mart*, a book we should probably all read.

I'm just as guilty about collecting "stuff." I can't seem to go to the Dollar Store without buying something. It's a bad habit. What am I going to do with all this stuff?

How much "stuff" do we need? We certainly can't take it with us when we die. We came into this world with nothing and I'm sure we'll leave the same way.

I doubt that my uncle got much pleasure out of worrying about his money. I know worrying about all my "stuff" and what's going to happen to it, when I die is only cause for grief. My mother worried more about people than she did "stuff." I know that she got a lot of pleasure out of helping people. Generous people, those who give of their time, talents and money are seldom sick. They are too busy giving to others to worry about themselves. Too immersed in the lives of others to think about themselves. That is a good thing (most of the time). Although there are always rare moments when you wished your parents spent more time fixing the mistakes in their own life and less meddling in yours!

According to a recent report, "Charitable giving in America has increased less than one percent in the past ten years. During this same time span, debt payments have risen 150 percent, while our entertainment is up 123 percent. Not surprisingly, the average consumer in this country spends $1.05 to $1.10 for every dollar of income." These figures are startling, even for a society where millions of people live in various degrees of debt. Something needs to change. (Internet report)

Giving should not be just an attitude; it needs to become a way of life. Some people are givers; others are takers – some are keepers. I knew growing up that I wanted to be just like my mother – a giver. When she died, she had one of the largest funerals I had ever attended up to that time. She was remembered not for her wealth but for her generosity, for her laughter and for her giving spirit. She was a friend to all who knew her. What a legacy to leave.

Chaotic Living…

The confusion of my life.

"Chaotic: living in utter confusion…" (Oxford American Dictionary) Yep, that pretty much describes my life.

After 27 years of living in the same house we decided to build a new one five miles down the road from our current house. Talk about utter confusion. Building the house itself was a time of bewilderment, but nothing compared to the actual move. If you have ever moved, you know what I'm talking about.

I stood in the middle of the kitchen one day surrounded by boxes; they were everywhere, with no clue as to what I was doing. I was unorganized and felt hopeless, lost amid the muck of moving.

"God," I cried out. "I need help!"

It wasn't more than five minutes that the phone rang. It was my friend, Betty.

"I know you're getting ready to move into your new house," she said. "I thought you could use a hand."

Isn't that just like God? Not only did he send a helper but he sent a woman who knew how to organize and pack boxes. She single-handedly tackled Bill's corner of the basement, sorted, cleaned, organized, packed (and labeled) most of his junk, making some sort of assembly out of the rubble that had once been our basement. Second, she boldly cleaned out kitchen cabinets pitching stuff that was at least 5 years old if not older. By the time she got done, basement, garage and kitchen were packed up and ready to go.

She reminded me that God is in us; we are His hands and feet. And she set her hands and feet to work. "The next time you need help," she said, "here, I am!"

Sometimes my life looks like my kitchen looked on moving day, unorganized in a chaotic state. But I have learned that if God can organize a kitchen He can certainly do something about the chaos in my life. He is a Savior who wants to bring order to our lives. All we need to do is ask for help.

In the upheaval that I sometimes find myself in, I simply go to my prayer closet and share my hectic life with God. But, remember if you are going to ask for help, be prepared to listen. My husband says that God doesn't talk to him. Of course God talks to him; he's just not listening. That's why we need to go to a quiet place so we won't be distracted by the noise in our lives. I love the quiet times I spend with God when I can share with Him what's really going on in my life. We get so busy that we often forget to spend time with God. One of the things I do to bring order to my life is to purposely plan to spend quality time with God. I sat aside time to talk to Him; beginning every day with prayer helps to restore order.

I'm a great list maker. I have to be, I'm old. If I don't make a list, I have no clue what I'm doing! I become easily distracted and forget things. Thank you God, for sticky notes! In order to bring a sense of balance back into my life, I make a list of things I need to accomplish. I had to do that in order to write this book. To discipline myself to write every day was on the top of my priority list (along with talking to God). I don't always get to everything on my list, but that's OK there is always tomorrow.

The important thing I do for myself is to submit to the will of God. Once I do that, well, me and God can accomplish just about anything!

Walking with God...

Or having tea as the case may be.

I was visiting a friend one-day who happened to be babysitting her four-year-old granddaughter, who appeared to be mumbling to herself. The granddaughter that is – not my friend. The little one was sitting at a child's play table set with teacups, happy as a lark.

"Who you talking, to, Sweetie?" I asked.

"I'm talking to God," she said. "We're having tea. Then we're going for a walk out in the backyard. Pooh is coming, too."

Isn't that sweet, I thought. She's having tea with God. I never thought about having tea with God but it sure seems like something nice to do.

On the way out to my car I couldn't help but notice the little girl (and Pooh) in the garden. She was still babbling. I drew closer without disturbing her and was surprised to find her praying. She was walking and talking with God about her day, her hopes and her dreams. My heart was stirred.

It reminded me of that old hymn, "I come to the garden alone, while the dew is still on the roses…and the voice I hear as I tarry there, none other has ever been known…"

Suddenly the little darling looked up and saw me watching her. She simply smiled, as if reading my mind. "He walks with me and He talks with me," she beamed.

And He tells me I am his own, I thought. Oh, to have the innocence and the faith of a little child again.

As I left that day, I promised myself that I would become like that little girl and that no matter what tomorrow brought, I'd spend some part of my talk walking and talking with God in the garden.

> "Man draws nearer to God as he withdraws from the consolations of this world."
> —*Thomas a Kempis*

Spreading the Good News…

By the "good" book or the "hard" fist

Our son has been sharing the good news of the gospel, that Jesus loves you since he was in second grade. He didn't always go about it rightly.

On two occasions, I caught him spreading the good news by hook and by fist. One day I got a call from the school principal that Matthew was preaching on the playground.

"That's not allowed," the principal said.

"Well, what's he doing?"

"He's telling the other children about Jesus and that if they don't accept Him, he'll have to beat them up!"

"Oh, is that all." A silent chuckle spread across my lips. "I'll take care of it," I assured. I couldn't help but wonder if the principal didn't have more important things to do than to worry about a little boy talking about Jesus?

After the supper meal, I sat Matthew down for a little talk. "You can't beat people over the head with the Bible," I explained to my son, trying to keep myself from keeling over with laughter. I mean the mere thought of it…our son preaching on the playground.

"Why not?" he wanted to know. "They need Jesus to save them…"

"Yes, I'm sure they do. But, you can only tell them about Jesus, Son, God has to do the saving. And we can't win souls to Christ by beating them up. You have to be patient and kind."

"Oh." He said. "I can try to do better."

That's all a mother could ask.

This little scenario did not scare him away.

The following winter, kids from across the ditch were taunting him. I heard him shout: "Jesus loves you!"

Whenever he got frustrated with life, he'd sing "Jesus loves me this I know…" He used the "What Would Jesus Do" slogan long before it became a popular expression.

He didn't stop sharing. As he grew, his love for Christ grew, too. He shared his faith and love for Christ in high school and in the work place.

When he was seven years old, our pastor told us that Matthew would end up doing some type of ministry. Not our son who'd rather use his fist than his words, who had a bad temper. Ministry didn't seem likely to me.

No one was more surprised than his father and I when our pastor announced from the pulpit one Sunday, youth in training and our son stood up. Today he and his wife head a Christian puppet ministry; they are active in kid's camp and other youth oriented programs. Matthew eventually learned to share his love for Christ with positive and encouraging words, (The fist didn't work) and he's good at it. Our pastor was right – he's ministering in a new and profound way. God is good.

The Value of a Good Argument

Only argue with the special people in your life.

I remember when I was a little girl the boys would pick on me. My mother told me it was because they liked me. She said people who don't care about one another don't bother arguing. "You only argue with special people," she said.

In college my daughter did a study on our family – she thought we were weird, I guess -- apparently, we are a family worth studying! My husband and I used to bet on whose family was the weirdest. His father was pretty eccentric, but so was my Aunt Helen! My Mom was loud, boisterous and often seemed controlling, but she was lovable and would shower you with hugs and kisses even in the face of an argument.

I came to realize in doing our family tree that every family is unique and every family tree needs a good trimming once in awhile.

My daughter said she worried about her father and I—all we do is argue. My mother said there is value in a good argument.

"Besides," I told my daughter. "Don't worry, your father and I argue over dumb stuff. When it comes to the really important things in life -- faith, family, morals -- we are of one accord."

"That's what my physchology professor said!" she laughed.

"Then I guess we're pretty normal, after all." I said.

Bill and I never disagreed on the value of family, raising our children or going to church. It didn't take our kids long to figure out that arguing was a form of communication for us.

There's a Russian proverb that says, "A mere friend will agree with you, but a real friend will argue." Bill and I argue all the time. I guess that makes him a friend worth arguing with.

I like that my friends and family trust me enough to argue. We can talk about work, family, hobbies and pastimes, even the Lord. Sometimes we don't always agree, but we always agree to disagree; there is no subject too big or small that isn't worth a good argument!

Gossip is Not Worth the Effort

Proverbs 16:28 says, "A gossip separates close friends." Truer words were never written. Nothing stings more or last longer than hurtful words spoken to you or about you. Someone's tittle-tattle can ruin a reputation, destroy a relationship or even kill a friendship. We forgive but we never forget the sting of hurtful words.

Listen to the news; read the newspaper. It seems as if the entire world runs on gossip. The media thrives on gossip; they feed on it; they keep the flame of moguls going. They sensationalize gossip in the name of freedom of speech.

Proverbs 6:16 says that God hates a lying tongue "…a false witness who utters lies, and one who spreads strife…" He'd rather see us exhorting one another, lifting one another up. (I Thessalonians 5:11) Saving the world with words of encouragement; feeding the lost with the good news of the gospel – not the good gossip of news.

We need to guard what comes out of our mouths. Think about the power of words. Be careful what we say to one another. A word that's been spoken is living not deed. Words have meaning, so say what you mean and mean what you say. Make your words count. Once a word has been spoken, you can't take it back. (From my book "*Bits and Pieces From My Mind)*

> "You are writing a gospel,
> A chapter each day.
> By deeds that you do,
> By words that you say.

Men read what you write,
Whether faithless or true,
Say, what is the gospel according to you?"
(From the book *Apples of Gold*)

The only way to settle a disagreement is not on the basis of who's right – but what's right. My mother was never bothered by gossip and she said I shouldn't be either, that as long as people are talking about me they aren't talking about someone else!

There's a field for critic's and gossipers, no doubt – but I have a feeling we'll never seen any of them in the Hall of Fame nor will God reward them by saying, "Well done good and faithful gossiper."

The Meek Shall Inherit the Earth...

The question is do I want the earth?

What does the meek shall inherit the earth mean? And considering the mess the world seems to be in, do I want to inherit the earth? What does it mean to be meek?

According to the Oxford American Desk Dictionary, to be meek means, "...to be humble, submissive, gentle in nature." Not something I'm good at.

The problem with humility and submissive is, the minute I think I've finally got it—I've lost it! I don't think you can be humble and wrapped up in yourself at the same time. I think that headstrong people have trouble with submissiveness—unless you are the one being submissive and they are the one expecting you to be submissive.

I decided to do a little research on "meekness". I found some interesting notions in regard to "meekness" in the book "*Apples of Gold*", thoughts on "meekness" that I've never consider until now.

Here's what I come up with so far. Meekness could mean to be ignorant of a great number of things. There are some things happening in this world where ignorance is actually bliss. I suppose that at some time or another we are all ignorant about something or other. Some people seem to confuse ignorance and meekness. To be gentle in nature is to avoid conflict and calamity. That kind of gentle nature is a good thing—not to be confused with being walked on and/or over—but to proceed through life in conflict and trauma with a spirit of kindness and gentleness. A kind word spoken gets better results than a word spoken in anger.

To be meek, could mean you're a person of resilience. I think resilience is an important factor in living life. It means that the winds of life no matter how strong they are cannot change who we are. We will not bend in the face of adversity, but will grow stronger and more confident because we will be resilient in spirit. No matter what storms come our way, we will survive.

I think to be humble is to know how to grow old in a graceful manner; to know when to concede without being conceited; to know when to back down; to teach thy tongue to say, "I don't know…I'm sorry…I won't do that again." To know God is to be humble.

To be submissive is a bit tougher and a little out of character for most of us. But an important attribute to have in a Christian, to be submissive to the Word of God is a good place to start your submissive training. There's a hundred ways I could describe what I think it means to be submissive. Swallowing your pride before it gives you indigestion is the first thing that comes to mind. Admitting you're wrong and submitting yourself to accepting someone else's ideas and opinions. Being submissive might mean not always being right.

Some people think they are philosophers. A philosopher is someone who always knows what to do until it happens to them. A humbly meek person is one who is willing to admit they're wrong. I don't mind admitting my faults; it makes me wiser than I was yesterday! And that's a good thing.

I don't know who said, "Humble is a man to have been a kid when everything was the kid's fault and to be a parent at a time when everything is the parent's fault…"but I like it. That takes humility my friend, and knowing how lucky you are in both circumstances!

One Day Time Stood Still

To touch a heart is to touch a life.

It seems like time is in control of everything we do. Clocks and watches run our lives; we have to be here, we have to be there. We are always looking at the clock making sure "it's time" or that "we'll be on time."

The following article titled "A Little Clock" came across my desk via of the Internet and first appeared in The Crossroads Newspaper, March 1999. It's a story that touched my heart. I'm hoping maybe it will touch yours, too.

A little clock in a jeweler's window in a small town stopped one day for half an hour at twenty minutes after eight. School children noticing the time stopped to play. People hurrying to the train looked at the clock and stopped to chat a little longer in the warm sunshine. All were late because one small clock stopped. Never had these people known how much they depended on that clock until it led them astray.

Many are thus unconsciously depending upon the influence of Christians. You may think you have no influence, but you cannot go wrong in one little act without leading others astray.

This message reminds of me that old Sunday school song: "This little light of mine, I'm going to let it shine" that I used to sing as a child. It makes me realize my light may be the only one shining in a dark world, and that what I do and what I say could influence someone's eternal life.

Time stands still for no man. Theologians have been preaching this for years. Christ is coming soon, my friends. He's no longer just around the corner or in the driveway – He's on the front porch! Perhaps, it's time to sing that song again, "This little light of mine, I'm going to let it shine," as a reminder that a dying world is depending on the influence of Christians.

(This article first appeared in The Crossroads Newspaper and then in His Banner Newspaper.)

Let God Carry the Potatoes

Sometimes you need help carrying the load.

I grew up on a farm. My dad planted mostly beans and corn, but Mother also had a small truck garden where she grew tomatoes, pickles and potatoes to sell at the Farmers Market in town.

When I was in high school I got a job baby-sitting for a potato farmer. When they needed help on the harvester, I'd pack up the kids and go out to the fields to help sort potatoes. Once in a basket, one person does not easily carry potatoes—they're heavy and often it takes two to carry the load.

It kind of works that way with God, too. Sometimes, you just can't carry the load by yourself – you need God's help.

There is a story of a poor man who plodded along toward home in a small Irish town carrying a huge bag of potatoes. A neighbor came along in a horse-drawn wagon and invited the man to climb inside. When the man sat down in the wagon he held the bag of potatoes in his arms.

When his neighbor suggests that he should set his load down, the old man said warmly, "I don't want to trouble you too much. You're giving me a ride, I'll carry the potatoes."

Sometimes we think we are doing the Lord a favor when we carry the burdens of life on our own. But the work his His, and He ask us only to be faithful in that which He has given us to do. I am like that poor old man. I appreciate the ride, but I don't want to trouble anyone so I carry the potatoes! When the load gets too heavy God wants to help us carry it.

(This article first appeared in The Crossroads Newspaper, August 1999.)

Patience is Not My Middle Name

But it is a virtue we all have.

When I really really want something badly, it's never time. In fact, I have a good friend, who is forever telling me, "Patience, my dear, it's not time, yet."

Patience is not my middle name. In spite of the fact that it is a Fruit of the Spirit mentioned in Galatians 5:22. (It's right up there with love, joy, peace, kindness and faithfulness,) I don't have it. I am not a very patient person, especially when I'm driving and find myself behind a Sunday driver! Of course, it's a different story when I'm the Sunday driver. One never realizes the importance of patience until faced with a situation where impatience seems to surface.

I found this article in the *Newsletter Newsletter* (May, 1997). It appropriately makes my point.

> A young woman's car stalled at a stoplight. She tried to get it started, but nothing happened. The light turned green and there she sat angry and embarrassed holding up traffic. The car behind her could have gone around her, but instead the driver added to her anger by lying on his horn.
>
> Another desperate attempt to start the car failed. The driver behind her kept honking. The frustrated woman got out of her car and walked to the honker. The man

rolled down his window in utter surprise.

"Tell you what," the woman said. "You go start my car and I'll sit back here and honk the horn for you."

We've all been there folks, but lying on the horn isn't going to help. As Christians, if we are going to live by the Spirit, we must also walk by the Spirit. Let us not become boastful, challenging one another, envious or angry. Where does that get us? And what does it prove? Only that we are of little patience. I am thankful God does not lose His patience with us, but continues to provide us with never ending grace.

Patience is a virtue. It's there for the asking. Once we get it, we need to practice using it!

(This article first appeared in The Crossroads Newspaper – September 1999.)

Things My Mother Thought I Should Know

(Thanks Mom!)

My mother lived through a lot of Mother's Day celebrations. When we are young we think mothers don't know much, but as we get older we realize just how smart they really are.

My mother showed me through her own experiences that in a matter of hours, people you don't even know can change your life. She taught me that a stranger is just a friend you haven't met yet. I've learned through the examples my mother set before me that even when you think you can't give any more you can always muster up the strength you need to help someone else. Whenever a friend needed her, Mom was there.

Mom taught me to consider my choices wisely, that decisions without thought can lead to heartache down the road, that anger incurs wrath and that kindness breeds love. "Always leave your family and friends with loving words," she told me. "It may be the last time you ever see them."

I remember tough times and rough roads and Mom teaching me that you can go on even when you think you are at the end of your rope. Mom said, "We are responsible for what we do—no matter how we feel."

Mom taught me that I am a hero, that heroes are people who get things done. I've learned to expect the best from myself and from others. I was taught to believe what people say, to take them at face value and give them the benefit of the doubt, that my word should mean something. I know that friendships don't just grow, they must be cultivated. I've learned that mothers can also be friends and that no matter how good a friend is, sometimes they hurt you, but that's what forgiveness is for and that in forgiving others, you must also learn to forgive yourself.

My mother managed to go through life with only an eighth grade education. I learned that although education is important a diploma hanging on the wall doesn't make you a decent human being—your mother does that!

As I have stood by and watched my parent's age, and saw my mother to her eternal reward, I came to the realization that the people we care about the most in life are taken from us too soon. I was not ready to let my mother go. I wish I could tell her just one more time, "Mom, I love you. Thank you for taking the time to instill your values in me and for teaching me not to take life for granted and for helping me to always remember the most important thing I can pass on to my children are love and laughter."

I didn't want to grow up to be just like my mother, but I'm glad I did!

(This article first appeared in The Crossroads Newspaper, May 2000.)

Successful Living is Easy

If you know the rules.

I've learned a little bit in 60 years. I learned that successful and healthy living is easy—if you know the rules. The rules are easier than you might think.

Give people more of yourself than they expect and do it cheerfully. Marry someone you love to talk to. As you get older, their conversational skills will be as important as any other skill, maybe more. And when you say, "I love you," mean it.

Don't believe everything you hear. In other words avoid gossip like the plague.

Spend all you have and sleep all you want. There's nothing wrong with an afternoon nap!

It's OK to admit you're wrong. When you say, "I'm sorry," look the person in the eye – and say it with conviction, like when you say, "I love you," mean it.

Believe in love at first sight; be engaged at least six month before you get married. Learning about one another is half the fun of the relationship.

People who don't have dreams don't have much, so when you dream, dream big! And never laugh at anyone else's dreams. Be a dream-maker not a dream buster.

Love deeply and passionately. You might get hurt but it's the only way to live life completely. Have a passion about and for the things you love.

Friends can agree to disagree. That's OK. In disagreements, fight fairly. No name-calling.

Don't judge people by their relatives—you could end up having those relatives in your family! Talk slowly but think quickly. Think with your heart and your head.

When someone asks you a question you don't want to answer, smile and ask, "Why do you want to know?"

Remember that great love and great achievements involve great risk; sometimes a risk is worth it. Remember with great power comes great responsibility!

Say "bless you" when you hear someone sneeze. Why not say "bless you" even if they don't sneeze. Blessings are good.

When you lose, don't lose the lesson learned. Make it work for you. Remember the three R's: Respect for self; respect for others, and take responsibility for all your actions.

Don't let a little dispute injure a great friendship. Don't let the sun go down on your anger. Never leave the room without offering a kind word. Never say goodbye, but see 'ya.

When you realize you've made a mistake, take immediate steps to correct it. Smile when picking up the phone. The caller will hear it in your voice. And most important, spend some time alone with God; listen to His voice and see what He has planned for your life.

(This article first appeared in The Crossroads Newspaper, November 2004.)

Making Words Count

Words to live by.

The tongue is a powerful weapon. The Bible refers to the tongue as a "two-edged sword." Ouch. Once words are spoken, they cannot be taken back and often they can leave a soul wounded beyond repair.

I, myself, have said and done things that I wish I wouldn't have. In fact, I probably do or say something I regret to someone, somewhere – every day. We really must learn to guard our words. What comes out of our mouths should be praise, first to God, and then to one another.

I hope you'll ponder these words of wisdom to live by:

Life is tough. Some days you're the pigeon, and some days you're the statue. There are days we are simply stuck in deep doo doo – no way to wiggle out—nothing we can do about it, other than to accept it.

Always keep your words soft and sweet, just in case you have to eat them! I find myself eating more "words" than I care too. And some of them taste awful!

Drive carefully. It's not only cars that can be recalled by their maker. And keep your driving words to yourself.

Eat a live toad in the morning and nothing worse will happen to you for the rest of the day. If you try this and it works – let me know!

If you can't be kind, at least have the decency to be vague, but purpose to practice kindness. Our world is in need of much kindness.

If you lend someone $20, and never see that person again, it was probably worth it. Sounds like good advice to me. My mother once told me, "Never lend money – just give it. That way if you get it back, it'll be a surprise."

It may be that your sole purpose in life is simply to serve as a warning to others. The best warning we can give is a warning of a life without Christ – not a good one.

Never buy a car you can't push. I've owned my share of cars you've had to push! I bought a car once that lasted two months – I was pushing it straight to the junkyard!

Never put both feet in your mouth at the same time, because then you don't have a leg to stand on. Need I say more?

Nobody cares if you can't dance well. Just get up and dance. If you don't know how to dance, learn. Life's too short not to enjoy it. So take full advantage of the beauty of life. Stop and smell the flowers, enjoy a gentle rain, watch for God's rainbows!

The early bird eats the worm--so sleep late. It's good to do that sometimes!

When everything's coming your way, you're probably in the wrong lane! If it's too good to be "true" it probably isn't!

Birthdays are good for you; the more you have, the longer you live. You may be only one person in the world, but you may also be the world to one person. That's why it's good to remember to encourage and praise one another. Your smile may be the only one that someone will see in a day. Some mistakes are too much fun to only make once.

Don't cry because it's over; smile because it happened.

We could learn a lot from crayons: some are sharp, some are pretty, some are dull, some have weird names, and all are different colors but they all have to learn to live in the same box. That's how we should look at life every day.

A truly happy person is one who can enjoy the scenery on a detour. When we travel and my husband makes a wrong turn and I say, "Great you've got us lost."

He assures me, "I'm not lost, I just don't know where I am, but God does!" We haven't been lost since we found Jesus.

Happiness comes through doors you didn't even know you left open. Never ever be afraid to open a new door – or to go through it. Something wonderful could be waiting on the other side.

(Thanks to my Internet friends in helping me to write this article.)

What's Up with "UP?"

Looking up is good.

There is a two-letter word that perhaps has more meaning than any other two-letter word in the dictionary, and that is the word, "UP." It's easy to understand UP, meaning toward the sky or at the top of the list, but when we wake in the morning, why do we wake UP?

At a meeting, why does a topic come UP? Why do we speak UP and why are officers always UP for election and please explain to me if you can, why is it UP to the secretary to write UP a report?

We read UP on a story in the paper that we pick UP to find out what's Up in the world and make UP our minds to not give Up hope that something good will eventually turn Up.

I don't know about you, but I call UP friends to say "hi," and when I'm cleaning, I brighten UP a room, polish UP the silver, and warm UP supper's leftovers and then, I clean UP the kitchen

We lock UP the house and some guys fix UP the old car. At other times that little word "UP" has real special meaning. People stir UP trouble, line UP for tickets, work UP an appetite, and think UP excuses for not cleaning out the garage or even going to church!

To be dressed is one thing but to be dressed UP is special, and this is confusing. A drain must be opened UP, because it is stopped UP. We open UP a store in the morning but we close it UP at night. We seem to be pretty mixed UP about UP.

To be knowledgeable of the proper uses of UP, look UP the word in the dictionary. In a desk size dictionary, UP takes UP almost 1/4th the page and definitions add UP to about thirty. If you are UP to it, you might try building UP a list of the many ways UP is used. This will take UP a lot of your time, but if you don't give UP, you may wind UP with Up to a hundred or more definitions on your list.

When it threatens to rain, we say it is clouding UP. When the sun comes out we say it is clearing UP. When it rains, it wets UP the earth. When it doesn't rain for a while, things dry UP. One could go on and on, but I'll wrap it UP, for my space here is limited and my time is UP. I'll leave it Up to you to step UP and keep Up the sharing of this list that has been made UP to lift Up your spirits. Have and UP lifting day! *(Thanks to my Internet friends for passing it on to me.)*

Camping is Taxing

If you don't understand the language.

God created the world in six days; on the seventh day He rested. I believe He intends for us to do the same, to take a break from the routine of everyday life. As our children were growing up, camping was one of our favorite things to do together. In spite of the fact that July is one of the hottest summer months (and campgrounds are crowded)--that's the month we'd pack up the tent and/or camper and head north for a week of camping. We don't do much camping anymore, but we still have a great time looking through the family album remembering what a wonderful time of our lives those carefree days of summer were.

Reserving a camp spot, however, was not nearly as fun as actually camping. In fact, making a campground reservation can be quite taxing, especially if you don't understand the language. The following story is a prime example and always makes me laugh.

My aunt is a rather old fashioned lady, quite delicate and very elegant, especially in the language she uses. (She is the only person I ever met who camped in her high heel shoes!) She and her friends were planning a week's vacation to a local campground. In making reservations, she wanted to make sure the campground was fully equipped, but didn't quite know how to ask about the toilet facilities. She just couldn't bring herself to write the word "toilet" in her letter. After much deliberation, she finally came up with the old fashioned term "bathroom commode," but on paper it looked much to forward so she simply referred to it as the B.C.

"…does the campground have its own B.C.," she wrote. Well, the manager of the campground had no idea what the woman was talking about and thought she surely must mean the location of the Baptist Church. He sat down and wrote the following reply:

Dear Madam,

    I regret very much the delay in answering your letter, but I now take pleasure in informing you that the B.C. is located nine miles north of the campground and is capable of seating 250 people at one time. I admit it is quite a distance away if you are in the habit of going regularly, but no doubt you will be pleased to know that a great number of people take their lunches along and make a day of it. They usually go early and stay late. The last time my wife and I went was six years ago. It was so crowded that we had to stand up the whole time we were there.

    It may interest you to know that right now there is a supper planned to raise money to buy more seats. They are holding it in the church basement. I would like to say it pains me very much not to go regularly, but it surely not to due to lack of desire on my part. As we grow older it seems to be more and more of an effort to go, particularly in the cold weather. If you decide to come down to our campground, perhaps, I could go with you the first time, sit with you and introduce you to all the other folks who go to the B.C.

    Remember, this is a very friendly community. I look forward to your visit to our campground and to the B.C.

Hope this little article brought a chuckle to your lips!

Pray For a Good Day...

And maybe you'll have one!

Sometimes I disappoint myself when I pray. I spend way more time than I should asking God for things instead of thanking Him for that which He has already given.

I think I need to spend less time complaining about how rotten this world is and more time praying for a good day. It may take some work, but I believe I can do it!

Praying for a good day isn't that hard. Just vow to start your day with happy thoughts. Make an effort to be agreeable and pleasing to the Lord.

Put a smile on your face—people like that! My mother used to tell me not to frown that my face would freeze that way and then what? Did you know it takes more effort (and you use more muscles) to frown than it does to smile? Mom could be right about the frowning thing.

Praying is the start to a good day. Take it one step further. Give someone a hug! Hugs are good therapy. Be kind to your pet. Call an old friend. Write a letter to your grandmother. Visit someone in a nursing home; you will realize what a good day you really are having!

Volunteer to mentor kids. Children keep you young and on your toes. (And, they keep you on your knees, too.) Help out a neighbor. Ask your pastor if he needs a hand in the church office.

Think about someone else other than yourself. You'll be surprised how fast your own problems disappear. Count your blessings one by one, you'll be totally amazed at what the Lord has done in your life. Most important, rejoice in the Lord, always.

Have a good day!

(This article first appeared in The Crossroads Newspaper, September 2000.)

God is Good…

All the time.

Have you ever been just sitting there and all of a sudden you feel like doing something nice for someone you care about? THAT'S GOD talking to you through the Holy Spirit.

Have you ever been so down and out and nobody seems to be around for you to talk to? THAT'S GOD waiting for you to talk to Him.

Have you ever been thinking about somebody that you haven't seen in a long time and the next thing you know you see them or receive a phone call from them? THAT'S GOD. There is no such thing as coincidence.

Have you ever received something wonderful that you didn't ask for, like money in the mail, a debt that had mysteriously been cleared, or a coupon to a department store where you had just seen something you needed, but couldn't afford to buy? THAT'S GOD knowing the desires of your heart.

Have you ever been in a situation and you had no clue how it was going to get better, how the hurting would stop, how the pain would ease, but now you look back on it and wonder why you worried about it? THAT'S GOD passing us through tribulation to see a brighter day, reminding us that joy comes in the morning!

God is great. God is awesome. What a mighty God we serve.
(This article appeared in His Banner Newspaper.)

"Happy is the man who has broken the chains which hurt the mind and has given up worrying once and for all."
—*Ovid*

What it Means to be Poor

Blessed are the poor in spirit.

One day a father of a very wealthy family took his son on a trip to the country with the firm purpose of showing his son how poor people can be. They spent a couple of days and nights on the farm of what would be considered a very poor family.

On the return trip, the father asked his son, "How was the trip?"

"It was great, Dad."

"Did you see how poor people can be?" the father asked.

"Oh Yeah," said the son.

"So, what did you learn from the trip?" asked the father.

The son answered, "I saw that we have one dog and they had four. We have a pool that reaches to the middle of our garden and they have a creek that has no end. We have imported lanterns in our garden and they have the stars at night. Our patio reaches to the front yard and they have the whole horizon. We have a small piece of land to live on and they have fields and fields that go beyond our sight. We have servants who serve us, but they serve others. We buy our food, but they grow theirs. We have walls around our property to protect us. They have lots of friends to protect them!"

With this the boy's father was speechless. Then his son added, "Thanks, Dad for showing me just how poor we really are."

Too many times we forget what we have and concentrate on what we don't have. What is one person's worthless object is another's prize possession. It is all based on our perspective of life and what makes us happy. Makes you wonder what would happen if we all gave thanks for all the bounty we have, instead of worrying about wanting more. Take joy in knowing that our heavenly Father has given us everything we could possibly want – and more!

Funeral Eulogy

What will your dash say about you?

A man stood to speak at the funeral of a dear friend. He referred to the dates on her tombstone - from the beginning to the end. He noted that first came her date of birth and spoke of the following date, his friend's death, with tears. But said the man, what mattered most of all is the dash between those years. (1900 - 1970)

For that dash represents all the time that my friend spent alive on earth and now only those who loved her know what that little line is worth.

For it matters not, how much we own; the cars, the house, the cash. What matters most is how we live and love and how we spend our dash.

So think about this long and hard. Are there things you'd like to change? For you never know how much time is left, that can still be rearranged.

If we could just slow down enough to consider what's true and real, and always try to understand the way other people feel. And be less quick to anger, and show appreciation more and love the people in our lives like we've never loved before.

If we treat each other with respect and more often wear a smile, remembering that this special dash might only last a little while.

So when your eulogy's being read with your life's actions to rehash, would you be proud of the things they say about how you spent your dash?

(This article first appeared in The Crossroads Newspaper and then in His Banner Newspaper.)

"Even the best writers talk too much."

—*Vauvenargues*

Is this YOU?

I have A.A.A.D.D.

I think I have A.A.A.D.D. - Age Activated Attention Deficit Disorder. This is how it manifests itself.

    I decided to wash my car. As I start toward to the garage, I notice that there is mail on the table. I decide to go through the mail before I wash the car.

    I lay my car keys down on the table, put the junk mail in the trash can under the sink, and notice that the trash basket is full.

    So, I decide to put the bills back on the table and take out the trash first but then I think, since I'm going to be near the mailbox when I take out the trash, anyway, I may as well pay the bills first. I take my checkbook off the table, and see that there is only one check left. My extra checks are in my desk in the office, so I go to my desk where I find the can of Diet Coke that I had been drinking.

    I'm going to look for my checks, but first I need to push the Diet Coke aside so that I don't accidentally knock it over. I see that the Diet Coke is getting warm, and I decide I should put it in the refrigerator to keep it cold.

    As I head toward the kitchen with the Diet Coke a vase of flowers on the counter catches my eye--they need to be watered. I set the Diet Coke down on the counter, and I discover my reading glasses that I've been searching for all morning. I decide I better put them back on my desk, but first I'm going to water the flowers.

    I set the glasses back down on the counter, fill a container with water and suddenly I spot the TV remote. Someone left it on the kitchen table. I realize that tonight when we go to watch TV, we will be looking for the remote, but nobody will remember that it's on the kitchen table. So I decide to put it back in the living room where it belongs, but first I'll water the flowers.

I splash some water on the flowers, but most of it spills on the floor. So, I set the remote back down on the table, get some towels and wipe up the spill. Then I head down the hall trying to remember what I was planning to do.

At the end of the day: the car isn't washed. The bills aren't paid. There is a warm can of Diet Coke sitting on the counter, the flowers aren't watered, and there is still only one check in my checkbook. I can't find the remote. I can't find my glasses, and I don't remember what I did with the car keys.

Then when I try to figure out why nothing got done today, I'm really baffled because I know I was busy all day long, and I'm really tired. I realize this is a serious problem, and I'll try to get some help for it, but first I'll check my e-mail.

Don't laugh - if this isn't you yet, your day is coming!
(Thanks to my Internet friends for helping me with this article.)

What God Didn't Promise...

God didn't promise days without pain, laughter without sorrow, sun without rain, but He did promise strength for the day, comfort for the tears, and light for the way.

God didn't promise that we'd never have disappointments. Disappointments are like road bumps, they slow you down a bit but you enjoy the smooth road afterwards. Don't stay on the bumps too long. Move on!

God didn't promise that you'd never have down days. When you feel down because you didn't get what you want, just sit tight and be happy, because God has thought of something better to give you.

God didn't promise that bad things would never happen. When something happens to you, good or bad, consider what it means.

God didn't promise you'd never cry. There's a purpose to life's events, to teach you how to laugh more or not to cry too hard. Ecclesiastics, Chapter Three, says, "There is an appointed time for everything...A time to laugh and a time to cry." (Verse 4)

God didn't promise that everyone you meet would love you. You can't make someone love you. All you can do is be someone who can be loved, and the rest is up to the person to realize your worth.

God didn't promise that you would never lose your pride. It's better to lose your pride to the one you love, than to lose the one you love because of pride.

God never promised that loving someone would always be

good. We spend too much time looking for the right person to love or finding fault with those we already love, when instead we should be perfecting the love we give.

God never promised that a friend would never leave you. Never abandon an old friend. You will never find one who can take his place. Friendship is like wine, it gets better as it grows older.

One thing I know for sure, God never promised me a rose garden! I know, my garden is full of dandelions!

What's the Moral?

Every good story has one.

I was sitting at a stop light one morning. The lady in front of me appeared to be going through papers or something on the seat of her car. When the light changed to green she did not obey its command - - a green light is a commandment – NOT a suggestion. Green means go.

When the light turned red, and she still had not moved, I began (with my windows up) screaming epithets and beating on my steering wheel. "The light is green. Go lady, go!" I was in a hurry. I needed to be somewhere five minutes ago! A policeman tapping on my window interrupted my expressions of distress. Against my protestations of "you can't arrest me for hollering in my car," he ordered me into the back seat of his car. This was not good.

After about two hours of trying to explain myself, the officer advised me I was free to go. I said, "I knew you couldn't arrest me for yelling in my own car. You shouldn't have even pulled me over. You haven't heard the last of this."

The officer replied, "I didn't pull you over for shouting in your car. I was directly behind you at the light. I saw you screaming and beating your steering wheel, and I said to myself, 'What a jerk. But there is nothing I can do to her for throwing a fit in her own car.'"

"So why did you pull me over then?"

"I noticed the "Cross" hanging from your rear view mirror, the bright yellow 'Choose Life' license tag, the 'Jesus is Coming Soon' bumper sticker, and the 'Fish' symbol, and I thought, "you must have stolen the car!"

The moral of this story - you won't win souls to Christ with your words (angry or otherwise,) but how you live your life. Perhaps, we all need a little more compassion and tolerance when waiting at a stoplight.

(Thanks to my Internet friends for helping me with this article.)

The Devil and the Duck

Don't play with slingshots.

A little boy was visiting his grandparents on their farm. He was given a slingshot to play with. He practiced in the woods, but he could never hit the target. Getting a little discouraged, he headed back for dinner.

As he was walking back he saw Grandma's pet duck. Just out of impulse, he let the slingshot fly, hit the duck square in the head, and killed it. He was shocked and grieved. In a panic, he hid the dead duck in the wood pile, only to see his sister watching! Sally had seen it all, but she said nothing.

After lunch the next day Grandma said, "Sally, let's wash the dishes." But Sally said, "Grandma, Johnny told me he wanted to help in the kitchen." Then she whispered to him, "Remember the duck?"

So Johnny did the dishes.

Later that day, Grandpa asked if the children wanted to go fishing and Grandma said, "I'm sorry but I need Sally to help make supper."

Sally just smiled and said, "Well that's all right because Johnny told me he wanted to help." She whispered again, "Remember the duck?"

So Sally went fishing and Johnny stayed to help.

After several days of Johnny doing both his chores and Sally's he finally couldn't stand it any longer. He came to Grandma and confessed he had killed the duck.

Grandma knelt down, gave him a hug, and said, "Sweetheart, I know. You see, I was standing at the window and I saw the whole thing. But because I love you, I forgave you. I was just wondering how long you would let Sally make a slave of you."

Thought for the day and every day thereafter:

Whatever is in your past, whatever you have done, and the devil keeps throwing it up in your face (lying, debt, fear, hatred, anger, unforgiveness, bitterness, etc.) whatever it is, you need to know that God was standing at the window and He saw the whole thing. He has seen your whole life. He wants you to know that He loves you and that you are forgiven. He's just wondering how long you will let the devil make a slave of you.

The great thing about God is that when you ask for forgiveness, He not only forgives you, but He forgets. It is by God's Grace and Mercy that we are saved. Go ahead and make the difference in someone's life today. Always remember that God is at the window!

(This article first appeared in The Crossroads Newspaper, 2002.)

"What Ifs and 'Ya Buts"

Don't fly with God.

When I was still working with my business partner, I had a million reasons why I couldn't or shouldn't do certain things. There was always a "ya but...what if this happened, or that happens? Ya but...I don't think it's going to work that way...ya but, what if God decides to do things a different way?" After several months of listening to my "ya buts" my partner gave me a dozen or so "ya but" coupons.

He said, "When these are going, you're done with the 'ya buts'."

It worked. I haven't used a "ya but" since!

And speaking of "what ifs"…

What if God couldn't take the time to bless us today because we couldn't take the time to thank Him yesterday?

What if God decided to stop leading us tomorrow because we didn't follow Him today?

What if we never saw another flower bloom because we grumbled when God sent the rain?

What if God didn't walk with us today because we failed to recognize it as His day?

What if God took away the Bible tomorrow because we would not read it today?

What if God took away His message because we failed to listen to the messenger?

What if God didn't send His only begotten Son because He wanted us to be prepared to pay the price for sin?

What if the door of the church was closed because we did not open the door of our hearts?

What if God stopped loving and caring for us because we failed to love and care for others?

What if God would not hear us today because we would not listen to Him?

What if God answered our prayers the way we answer His call to service?

What if God met our needs the way we give Him our lives?

Please don't give God any "ya buts" – they won't work with Him, either.

Count Your Blessings...

See what God's doing in your life.

The world seems to be full of whiners and complainers – and why not. The way things are going, there's a lot to complain about!

Still, when you stop to think about it, there is a lot more to be thankful for than to complain about. Perhaps, if we spent more time counting our blessings and less time complaining, we'd see just how much we have to be grateful for.

As Christians when we allow our complacent spirit to surface, daily blessings slip away unnoticed. When we start our day grumbling and continue to fuss about nothing, we often end up ignoring God and never see the things He's blessed us with.

Personally speaking, I missed out on some pretty awesome blessings because I was too busy whining and complaining and don't notice them. Blessings are like, sunlight peering through the trees; raindrops dancing on the windowsill, walking in the rain! Sitting on the deck, thinking, meditating on the Word. Smelling roses along the lane, picking wildflowers and giving them away—just because.

Today is the day He wants to bless you with a new song in your heart and a smile on your lips. Why? Because He wants you to pass it along to someone in need of a gentle touch.

So, what's God doing in your life? Instead of complaining, STOP, count your blessings, and name them one by one. I'm sure as that old hymn says, "You'll be surprised to see what the Lord hath done."

(This article appeared in The Crossroads Newspaper – October 1999.)

"A hero is no braver than an ordinary man, but he is brave five minutes longer."
—*Ralph Waldo Emerson*

Dad, A Three Letter Word for Hero

Some time ago I wrote the following tribute to fathers as a reminder to remember our dads not only on Father's Day but every day. To let him know how much he is appreciated is according to my father "reward enough on any day."

The Bible tells us to honor thy father and thy mother. Kids News did a survey on heroes some years ago. In spite of the statistics that say fathers do not spend enough time with their children, 70 percent of kids ages 10 through teens interviewed, when asked, "who their hero is," said, "my dad."

They gave various reasons: "He's my role model. "He taught me everything I need to know about life." "He talks to me about important things." "He loves me even when I mess up." "I know he'll always be there when I need him—no matter what." "I look up to my dad; he's honest, fair and forgiving." "He saved me from a burning building—he's my hero." "My dad is my hero because he tells me that he loves me every day."

Friends, it seems fitting that we should pay tribute to our fathers – not just on Father's Day but every single day. We shouldn't let a day go by that we don't tell Dad, "I love you." God doesn't always give us the father we want, but he always gives us the father we need!

My dad was a busy man when I was growing up. Not only was he a farmer but he worked in a factory, too. Sometimes he didn't have time for a story or a picnic, but he always had time for a hug. I can truthfully say I got the father I wanted and needed.

My dad is in his 90s now so I want to be sure to say, "Thanks Dad, for always being there when I need you."

(This article first appeared in The Crossroads Newspaper – June 2000.)

Most Embarrassing Moments

I never have embarrassing moments. I have moments to remember! Or should I say moments I can't forget.

My first such moment was age 11. I had just gotten a new bike for my birthday. I wanted to take it for a spin down the road.

"You better changed out of your Sunday clothes, first." My mother instructed.

It was almost time for dinner. I didn't have time to change my clothes. Besides, I wasn't going far…just down the road. How long would that take? I'd be back before anyone knew I was gone.

Choosing to ignore my mother's advice, down the road I went on my new blue bike, happily humming, peddling as fast as I could. I glanced down at my watch to make sure I had enough time to get home for dinner, lost my balance and drove straight into the ditch!

There I was at the bottom of murk and mud with my brand new bike on top of me! This was embarrassing. How was I going to explain this to my mother?

Everyone was sitting at the dinner table as I limped into the house, hair a mess, dress torn. My paten leather shoes ruined! Embarrassed was not the word for what I was feeling.

My mother simply pointed to her watch and said, "You're late for dinner." Not another word was uttered. No one bothered to ask if the bike was OK.

We've all had those terrible embarrassing memories, under slip showing, coming out of the restroom with toilet paper stuck to your shoe. Tripping as you go up the stage to receive your diploma. Getting the hair brush stuck in your hair and sitting there crying about it. Remember Heidi? I can beat that.

Nothing was as embarrassing to me as the day I fell off the exam table at the OBGYN'S office.

Imagine, if you will, one minute I was sitting on the table with that thin paper white sheet over me, and the next thing I knew I was on the floor. The doctor, who was more embarrassed I think than I was trying, without touching me, to help me up. My hands and legs flailing in every direction; paper gown on the floor. Oh yes, I was stark naked. Well, not totally naked. I had my fun socks on!

I don't think the good doctor noticed that the socks were fun; he was a bit stressed out; trying to help me with his eyes closed wasn't working.

That's when his nurse assistant arrived on the scene looking more horrified than I felt.

"Oh my…OK then…I'll come back when you're ready, Doctor." She backed out the door. "I'll give you a moment."

Don't give me a moment! I wanted to shout. I don't need a moment!

"Help" was the exasperated look on the doctor's face. He didn't need a moment either, except maybe a moment to forget what just happened here. And what did happen? I'm not sure. I just know I didn't want it to happen again.

And apparently neither did the doctor. The next time I made a visit to his office, I found myself sitting on a new low-to-the floor exam table made for those with disabilities, physical problems – and midgets!

Another embarrassing moment that stands out in my mind was coming into a church for a funeral realizing half way through the eulogy that I was in the wrong church.

"God bless you," I said as I made my way through the receiving line out the door to my car. Carefully, I removed that little funeral flag and drove away before anyone realized that I didn't know the dearly departed. I was sorry I missed the funeral dinner. Pat would have wanted me there, I'm sure!

And speaking of Pat. Have you ever run into someone who seems to know you but you can't remember who they are? If so, just ask them how Pat is doing. (Not the Pat that died, of course). Everyone seems to know a Pat.

"Connie! Hi, how are you?" An acquaintance from my past flags me down at the Mall.

"I'm fine. It's so good to see you again." I had no idea who I was talking to.

"How's the family?"
"Just fine," I said.
"And yours?"
"Great." My old newly found, old friend said.
"And how's Pat?" I sheepishly asked for want of something more to say.
"I'm Pat," she said.

Well, it works for me most of the time. Maybe it'll work for you, most of the time, too!

"Faith is the soul riding at anchor."
—*Josh Billings*

Who Put the "X" in X-ray?

I have been battling with a painfully annoying heel spur. Our pastor reminds us that we should seek the wise counsel of our physicians, but not to neglect praying over our situation for God after all is still in the healing business. And the prayer of a righteous man availeth much.

I decided to take his advice and consult both God and my doctor! The first thing my foot doctor did was to x-ray my heel. This was followed by not one but two cortisone injections. (Ouch! Yes, big girls do cry.)

However, sitting in that chair fighting to be brave made me think about x-rays and how they got their name. After I left the doctor's office, hobbling, I decided to do a little research on the subject of x-rays and found that in 1895, German inventor, Wilhelm Roentgen was conducting experiments with the conduction of electrical charges through gases in a vacuum tube. Much to his astonishment, Roentgen observed that radiation passed through objects that were usually opaque. The applications were obvious, but Roentgen didn't understand how or why radiation worked. For this reason, Roentgen named his invention x Strahlen (X-ray). He used "X" as in algebraic formulas, a modest admission that he couldn't explain his own discovery.

I have no reason for passing this information on to you other than to kill time while I'm waiting for my heel spur to heal. Perhaps, I need to take my pastor's advice and spend more time in prayer (knee-mail – God loves it!).

Oh, thanks to my friend Betty for giving me the book *Who Put The Butter in Butterfly? (And other fearless investigations into our illogical language)* by David Feldman. Both Mr. Feldman and Betty helped me in writing this story!

(This article first appeared in The Crossroads May 2004.)

"Children are hopes."
—*Novalis*

Life's Choices

Have you ever met one of those real positive people? You know the one who gets up in the morning singing! I hate that. I'm not a morning person, but I remember as a child, my mother was one of those people. A morning singer – my mother and the birds!

I have a friend who is always in a good mood. No matter what's happening, my friend always has something positive to say. When someone says, "Hi, how are you doing?" The answer is always the same, "Great!" How can you be "great" all the time?

It makes me wonder how I can become a natural motivator?

According to my friend, it's not that hard. In fact, it's easy. All you have to do is STOP and DUMP.

Stop whining. Look for the positive in every situation.

Dump the grumps! Smile, hum—sing! Do whatever it takes to turn your life around.

Stop making bad choices. Each morning you wake up, say to your self, "Self, you have two choices today. You can be in a good mood or you can choose to be in a bad mood." Direct your heart to choose a good mood.

Stop gripping and learn. Every time something bad happens, you can choose to be a victim or, you can choose to learn from your mistakes.

Dump the complaints! God hates whiners and complainers. And don't let anyone else complain either. When someone comes to you complaining, you can choose to accept it or point out the positive side of life. Negative personalities hate that!

Living a positive life is easy once you realize that it's all about choices.

Dump the junk in your life. Cut through all the garbage by

choosing how you react to life's situations, to the people in your life. Stop being an enabler. I'm good at that one.

The bottom line is: Life is about the choices you make; how you respond to every day life is really up to you!

In running my own business the word CHOICES surfaced many times in the course of a day. I often found myself stopping and dumping. I've come to realize that our attitudes are everything. They determine success or failure.

If all else fails, memorize Matthew 6:34 "Therefore do not worry about tomorrow, tomorrow will take care of itself. Each day has enough troubles of its own." That makes good sense to me. After all, today is the tomorrow we worried about yesterday and what good did that do? We should focus more on making good choices — on stopping and dumping!

It's not easy being a Christian

It's not easy being a Christian. I know I said this already but God never promised us a rose garden, but more a rock garden! Roses are beautiful, but they don't come without thrones. And rock gardens are lovely, but they take work and believe it or not, it's harder to keep the weeds out of a rock garden.

I get a warm, bubbly feeling when I see a group of Christians singing and shouting and praising His name. It's the greatest feeling in the world to know that you're saved, sanctified and filled with the Holy Ghost, but I'm smart enough to know there's more to being a Christian than what meets the eye.

I think the following poem that came across my computer screen via of the Internet says it best:

When I say, "I am a Christian"

When I say, "I am a Christian"
I'm not shouting, "I am saved"
I'm whispering "I was lost!"
That is why I chose this way."

When I say, "I am a Christian"
I don't speak of this with pride.
I'm confessing that I stumble
And need someone to be my guide.

When I say, "I am a Christian"

I'm not trying to be strong.
I'm professing that I'm weak
And need help to carry on.

When I say..."I am a Christian"
I'm not bragging of success.
I'm admitting I have failed
And cannot ever pay the debt.

When I say..."I am a Christian"
I'm not claiming to be perfect,
My flaws are too visible
But God believes I'm worth it.

When I say..."I am a Christian"
I still feel the sting of pain.
I have my share of heartaches
Which is why I seek His name.

When I say..."I am a Christian"
I do not wish to judge.
I have no authority.
I only know I'm loved.

(Author unknown)

I am so glad that I belong to Christ. What a blessing it is to know that no matter what I do in this life He loves me!
(This article first appeared in The Crossroads March 2000.)

Saying I Love You

The one thing about writing a book is coming up with an appropriate ending to the book – knowing when to stop. I decided I wanted to end on a love note. God's great commandment is to love one another. It seems like the only time we really think about the value and merit of love is in February. It's a month that seems to spell V-A-L-E-N-T-I-N-E-S Day, a time when a young man's fancy turns to love.

Wait a minute-that's spring. Valentine's Day is that one-day of the year when we are suppose to tell one another "I love you." Easier said than done for most of us.

Jesus said we are to love one another even as He loved us. His intention for us to love one another was not just for one day a year, but for every day. I was thinking about how wonderful the world would be if mankind just took time to "love", unconditionally as Christ loves us. Those three little words "I love you" could change someone's life. For those of you who are struggling with that thought, here is a dozen ways of saying, "I love you."

> Cambodian; Bon sro lanh oon
> Chinese: Wo ai ni
> French: Je t'aime
> German: Ich liebe dich
> Greek: S'agapo
> Hebrew: Ani ohev otahk
> Hungarian: Szretlek
> Italian: Ti voglio bene
> Norwegian: Diego esker Deem
> Polish: Kochem cie

Russian: Ya vas luibliu
Spanish: Te quiero

No matter what language you speak love in; the important thing is to let someone know you care. If you're having trouble pronouncing any of the above, then just live the meaning of it! And men don't forget Valentine's Day-it's a no no. In fact celebrating Valentine's Day every day is a "yes yes" for everyone in your life!
(*This article first appeared in The Crossroads Feb. 2001)*

I hope there will be many more books. I love you for buying this one. Thank you!

Connie Hawkins

www.ingramcontent.com/pod-product-compliance
Lightning Source LLC
Chambersburg PA
CBHW061655040426
42446CB00010B/1751